CHOCOHOLIC

**50 irresistible indulgences:
the ultimate cook's collection**

CHOCOHOLIC

Elizabeth Wolf-Cohen

Photography by Edward Allwright

southwater

This edition is published by Southwater

Distributed in the UK by
The Manning Partnership
251–253 London Road East
Batheaston
Bath BA1 7RL
tel. 01225 852 727
fax 01225 852 852

Published in the USA by
Anness Publishing Inc.
27 West 20th Street
Suite 504
New York
NY 10011
fax 212 807 6813

Distributed in Canada by
General Publishing
895 Don Mills Road
400–402 Park Centre
Toronto, Ontario M3C 1W3
tel. 416 445 3333
fax 416 445 5991

Distributed in Australia by
Sandstone Publishing
Unit 1, 360 Norton Street
Leichhardt
New South Wales 2040
tel. 02 9560 7888
fax 02 9560 7488

Southwater is an imprint of Anness Publishing Limited
Hermes House, 88–89 Blackfriars Road, London SE1 8HA
tel. 020 7401 2077; fax 020 7633 9499

© 1994, 2001, 2002 Anness Publishing Limited

Publisher: Joanna Lorenz
Senior Editor: Lindsay Porter
Editor: Gillian Haslam
Designer: Peter Laws
Jacket designer: The Bridgewater Book Company Limited
Photographers: Edward Allwright
Stylist: Maria Kelly

Previously published as *Step-by-Step Cooking with Chocolate*

CONTENTS

INTRODUCTION

Chocolate, one of the world's most well-loved foods, is enjoying an all-time popularity. It is an ingredient with a long and impressive pedigree: for centuries the Aztecs drank a bitter, frothy drink called 'chocolatl', made of roasted cocoa beans mixed with water or wine. Cocoa beans were then introduced to Europe in the sixteenth century, and cocoa became a food of kings. Its true potential was not exploited until the early nineteenth century when the chocolate press was invented in Holland, but from that point onwards, chocolate has gone from strength to strength. It is now available in countless forms and varieties, and is used as a flavouring in every conceivable dessert and sweet — bitter chocolate is even used in some savoury dishes.

This book is for all lovers of chocolate. It contains a glorious array of fabulous desserts and sweet indulgences — cakes, pies, tortes, mousses, ice creams, cookies, brownies, muffins and truffles galore — using chocolate in every guise. The recipes are special enough to share with friends, or give as gifts, but be sure to make an extra batch to enjoy yourself — they are truly irresistible.

Types of Chocolate

Chocolate is found in many different forms, ranging from solid to pre-melted, from extra dark to white, from unsweetened to sweet and milky. All chocolates, even those of the same type, taste different, depending on the quality and roasting of the cocoa beans, the quality and style of production and the national tastes of the country in which the chocolate has been manufactured.

Eating and cooking chocolates are made from chocolate liquor which is blended with extra cocoa butter, sugar and flavourings. The more chocolate liquor (mass or solids) and butterfat the chocolate contains, the higher the quality. Although certain types of chocolate lend themselves to certain preparations, chocolate is very much a personal preference.

Chocolate chips

Originally produced by chocolate manufacturers in the US for use in chocolate chip cookies, these pieces are available in various sizes and as bittersweet, semi-sweet, milk and white. Because they are designed to keep their shape in a variety of baked goods, they are best used in recipes like cookies, cakes and confections. Although they can be melted, they contain less cocoa butter than ordinary chocolate.

Cocoa

Cocoa is the pure chocolate mass which is left when the cocoa butter has been removed from the chocolate liquor. Ground and sifted, cocoa gives the most intense chocolate flavour to baked goods and desserts.

Dutch-processed cocoa or Dutch cocoa is neutralized by a process called 'Dutching', giving the cocoa a darker, reddish colour but a slightly milder flavour. This is sometimes called European-style cocoa, as almost all imported cocoas are Dutch-processed or 'natural'.

cocoa

Non-alkalized cocoa which is commonly available in the US has a sharper flavour because the acids are left untreated. Unless specified, the two types can be interchanged although the flavour of 'natural' cocoa will be more intense. In baking, cocoa should be sifted into the dry ingredients or diluted with boiling water to form a paste, much like cornflour, before being added to other mixtures.

Drinking chocolate or other hot or cold chocolate commercial preparations are made from cocoa to which sugar and sometimes dried milk solids have been added.

Couverture or covering chocolate

This is a very fine, richly-flavoured chocolate which has a high proportion of cocoa butter, giving it a glossy appearance and smooth fluid texture. It is expensive and mostly used by professionals for coating and dipping other chocolates. This chocolate must be 'tempered' (see page 12). It is available in some speciality shops or by mail order as bittersweet, semi-sweet, milk or white chocolate.

Although it can be used when a very fine flavour and texture are required, it is not generally used in baking or desserts. Do not confuse couverture with commercial coating chocolate or cake covering, made with the addition of other fats and oils, which are cheaper and easier to use, but lack the flavour and gloss of fine couverture.

chocolate chips

couverture chocolate

plain chocolate

unsweetened chocolate

White chocolate

Technically, white chocolate is not chocolate at all because it contains no chocolate liquor. It is a commercial product made from cocoa butter, milk and sugar. In the US it is called a confectionery coating and some white chocolate may contain vegetable fat as well as, or instead of, cocoa butter, so read the label carefully. White chocolate has recently become very popular and is used in mousses, cakes and sauces and as a contrast to other chocolates. As with milk chocolate, it is sensitive to heat, so be very careful when melting it. Use a double boiler or water bath and keep the temperature between 225–250°F/110–120°C.

Plain, bittersweet and semi-sweet chocolate

These types of chocolate contain only chocolate liquor, cocoa butter and sometimes lecithin (an emulsifier), sugar and vanilla in varying quantities. Each country has different guidelines for the content of cocoa solids, which accounts for the wide variety in quality. In the US chocolate must contain 34% solids and in the UK 35%. Best results in cooking are obtained with chocolate which contains a minimum of 50% chocolate solids. The recipes specify one of these types, but you may substitute one type for another and use, for example, a more bitter chocolate if you prefer a less sweet flavour.

Unsweetened chocolate

Also known as 'Bakers' chocolate' or 'bitter chocolate' (not bittersweet), unsweetened chocolate is the cooled chocolate liquor blended with a quantity of cocoa butter. It contains no sugar, has a bitter, full chocolate flavour and is used mainly in manufacturing chocolate products. Used widely in the US and Canada in baking because of its intense flavour, it is difficult to find in the UK. For baking, an adequate substitute for 30 g/1 oz unsweetened chocolate is 20 g/¾ oz/3 tbsp cocoa plus 15 g/½ oz/1 tbsp unsalted butter. The sugar in the recipe must also be adjusted according to the recipe.

Milk chocolate

Milk chocolate is made with dried milk powder. It has a much milder, more creamy flavour than dark chocolate and cannot be substituted for bittersweet or dark chocolate in baking and dessert recipes because it has a lower cocoa solid content. Extra care should be taken when melting it.

white chocolate

milk chocolate

Equipment

The only chocolate work requiring specialized equipment is moulding. Other equipment can be improvised.

Baking sheets
Heavy duty, non-stick baking sheets make baking easier.

Cake tester
A thin metal skewer used for testing cakes.

Chocolate moulds
Available in many shapes, plastic moulds are easy to use.

Chocolate tools
The triangle and dipping fork are used for coating chocolates and truffles. A kitchen fork can be used.

Cutters
A selection of different shaped cutters is useful.

Double boiler
Useful for melting chocolate and cooking custards.

Ice cream scoop
A small scoop is ideal for biscuit mixtures and truffles.

Instant-read thermometers
Very useful in chocolate and sugar work.

Marble slab
Provides a cold surface for pastry and chocolate work.

Measuring spoons
Essential for accurate measuring of ingredients.

Palette knife
A metal palette knife is useful for removing goods from baking sheets, spreading creams and fillings.

Pastry bag and tips
A selection is essential for decorating and piping.

Springform tins
Used to make desserts which cannot be inverted for unmoulding. The clip-on side forms a tight seal.

Sugar thermometer
Used to measure high temperatures when cooking sugar.

Swivel-bladed peeler
Used for peeling fruits, removing citrus zest and making chocolate curls.

Tart tins
Choose a good quality metal tin with a removable bottom for easy unmoulding.

Wooden skewers
Used for testing cakes and moving delicate ingredients such as chocolate curls.

double boiler

flour dredger

sieves

swivel-bladed peeler

palette knife

kitchen knife

pastry bags and tip

kitchen scissors

kitchen plates

chopping board

marble slab

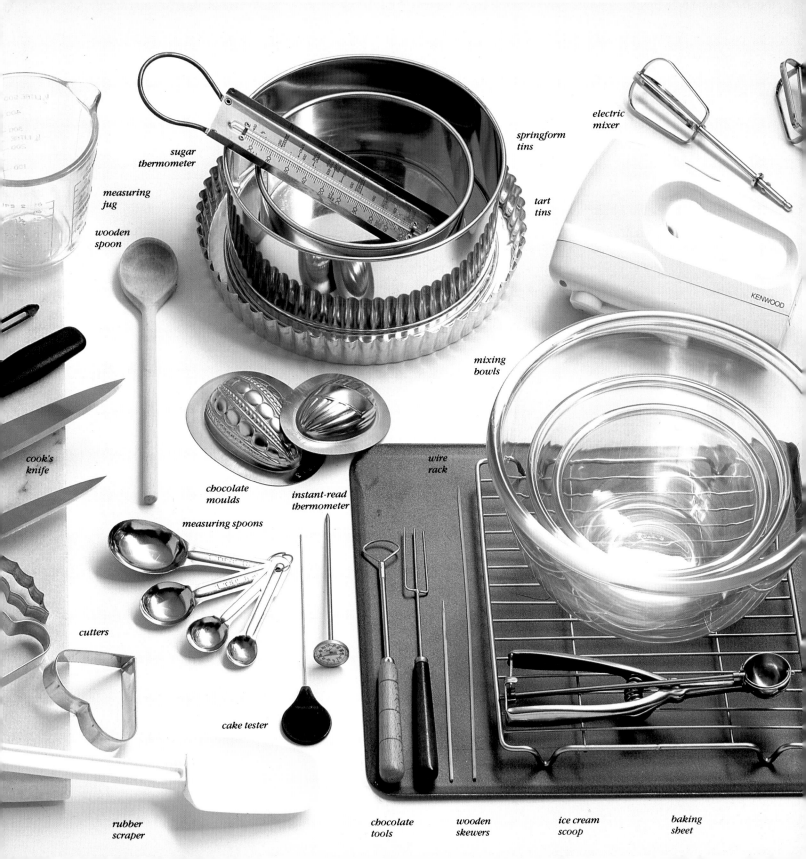

sugar
thermometer

measuring
jug

wooden
spoon

springform
tins

electric
mixer

tart
tins

KENWOOD

mixing
bowls

cook's
knife

chocolate
moulds

instant-read
thermometer

wire
rack

measuring spoons

cutters

cake tester

rubber
scraper

chocolate
tools

wooden
skewers

ice cream
scoop

baking
sheet

Choosing and Storing Chocolate

Before buying chocolate, check the recipe and use what the recipe calls for; always buy the best quality of its type.

In general, all chocolate should be kept in its original wrapper if possible, or wrapped in foil and then plastic. Store in a cool, dry place at about 18°C/65°F. Do not store chocolate in the refrigerator. High humidity will shorten the shelflife of chocolate. Unsweetened and dark chocolates will keep for years in ideal conditions. Milk chocolate will keep for up to a year, and white chocolate, because of its high butterfat content, will keep for 6–8 months. Certain chocolates, such as couverture and bittersweet chocolate, as well as prepared chocolates such as truffles, freeze well.

Incorrectly stored chocolate will 'bloom'. 'Sugar bloom' occurs when chocolate is exposed to moisture. As the moisture evaporates, it draws out tiny particles of sugar, leaving the surface looking 'mouldy'. 'Fat bloom' occurs when the chocolate has become too warm. The cocoa butter begins to melt and forms greyish-white areas on the surface.

Although unattractive, bloom does not affect the flavour and the chocolate can still be used.

Cooking with Chocolate

If chocolate is being melted alone, all the equipment must be *completely dry* as water may cause the chocolate to thicken and become a stiff paste. For this reason, do not cover chocolate during or after melting it as condensation could form. If chocolate does thicken, add a little pure white vegetable fat (not butter or margarine) and mix well. If it does not work, start again. Do not discard chocolate: it may be used in a recipe where the chocolate is melted in another liquid.

Chocolate can be melted with a liquid, but there must be sufficient liquid. If melted with butter, cream, milk, water, coffee or a liquid that is unlikely to burn, generally 15 ml/1 tbsp of liquid to each 60 g/2 oz of chocolate should be safe, but if the chocolate appears to be thickening, add more liquid.

With or without liquid, chocolate should be melted *very slowly*. It is easily burned or scorched and overheated chocolate can turn gritty and develop a poor flavour. Dark chocolate should not be heated above 50°C/120°F. Milk and white chocolates should not be heated above 45°C/110°F.

Tempering Chocolate

Tempering is the process of gently heating and cooling chocolate to stabilize the emulsification of cocoa solids and butterfat. This technique is generally used by professionals with couverture chocolate. It allows the chocolate to shrink quickly (to allow easy release from a mould, for example with Easter eggs) or to be kept at room temperature for several weeks or months without losing its crispness and shiny surface. All solid chocolate is tempered in production, but once melted loses its 'temper' and must be re-tempered unless it is to be used immediately.

Untempered chocolate tends to 'bloom' or becomes dull and streaky or takes on a cloudy appearance. This can be avoided if melted chocolate is refrigerated immediately as chilling the chocolate solidifies the cocoa butter and prevents it from rising to the surface or 'blooming'. General baking and dessert-making do not require tempering, which is a relatively fussy procedure and takes practice. However, it is useful when preparing sophisticated decorations, moulded chocolates or coatings. Most shapes can be made without tempering if they are refrigerated immediately.

1 Melt the couverture chocolate by the preferred method – the microwave method is quick, easy and the least messy. The temperature should be about 45°C/110°F. Stir to be sure the chocolate is completely melted and smooth.

2 Pour about three-quarters on to a marble slab or baking sheet and, using a metal palette knife or rubber scraper, quickly scrape into a pool in the centre and then spread out again. Work the chocolate for 3–5 minutes until no streaks remain. Scrape back into the chocolate remaining in the bowl and stir until blended. The temperature should be about 32°C/90°F. The chocolate is now tempered and ready for use.

Double Boiler Method

This is probably the most traditional method of melting chocolate.

1 If you do not have a double boiler, place a small heatproof bowl over a saucepan. Make sure the bowl fits snugly so no water or steam can splash into it. Do not allow the water in the bottom of the double boiler or saucepan to come to a boil.

2 Place the broken or chopped chocolate in the double boiler top or bowl and place over double boiler bottom or saucepan. Lower the heat as much as possible, or turn it off completely, and allow the chocolate to melt slowly, stirring frequently.

Direct Heat Method

When a recipe directs melting chocolate with a liquid such as milk, cream or even butter, it can be done over direct heat in a saucepan.

1 Choose a heavy-bottomed saucepan and melt the chocolate and liquid over low heat, stirring frequently, until chocolate is melted and smooth. Remove from heat immediately. This method is also used for making sauces, icings and some sweets.

2 Chocolate can also be melted in a very low oven (about 110°C/225°F/Gas ¼). Put the chocolate in an ovenproof bowl and place in the oven for a few minutes. Remove the chocolate before it is completely melted and stir until smooth.

Microwave Method

The microwave is ideal for melting chocolate quickly and easily, but remember to check it during the cooking time.

Grated Chocolate

Chocolate can be grated by hand or in a food processor. Make sure you grate it at the correct temperature.

1 Chill the chocolate and hold it with a piece of folded foil or paper towel to prevent the heat of your hand melting it. Hold a hand or box grater over a large plate and grate the amount of chocolate required.

1 Place chopped or broken chocolate in a microwave-safe bowl and microwave on MEDIUM power (50%) for about 2 minutes for 115 g/4 oz dark, bittersweet or semi-sweet chocolate. Milk and white chocolate should be melted on LOW power (30%) for about 2 minutes for 115 g/4 oz of chocolate.

2 These times are for a 650–700 W oven and are *approximate* times as both chocolate and microwave ovens vary, so check the chocolate about halfway through cooking time. The chocolate does not change shape, but begins to look shiny and must then be stirred until completely melted and smooth.

Be Careful

Chocolate can burn in the microwave, so be sure to check frequently and continue to microwave at 5–10 second intervals if chocolate has not melted sufficiently.

Chocolate melted with liquid or butter may melt more quickly if the liquid has a high fat content, so check the chocolate frequently.

2 A food processor fitted with the metal blade can also be used to grate chocolate, but be sure the chocolate is soft enough to be pierced with a sharp knife. Cut the chocolate into small pieces and, with the machine running, drop the chocolate pieces through the feed tube until grated. This produces very fine shavings. Alternatively, use the grater attachment and pusher to feed the chocolate through the processor for larger shavings.

Coating with Chocolate

Truffles, caramels and other sweets, as well as fresh or dried fruit pieces, can all be coated in chocolate. Tempered couverture chocolate is the ideal method, but melted bittersweet or semi-sweet chocolate can be used if the chocolate is refrigerated immediately.

1 Melt the chocolate by the preferred method and pour into a bowl deep enough to cover whatever is being coated. The temperature should be about 46°C/115°F but not above 50°C/120°F. Use a fondue fork, skewer or special chocolate dipping fork to lower the sweet into the chocolate. Turn to coat completely and lift out of the melted chocolate, tapping gently on the edge of the bowl to remove excess chocolate.

2 Place on a non-stick baking paper-lined baking sheet, and if you like, draw the tines of the dipping fork across the top, lifting lightly to leave two raised ridges.

Solid Easter Eggs

To fill 4 egg shells, melt 450 g/16 oz of chocolate. Couverture chocolate should be tempered. Decorate the eggs with ribbon or coloured foil.

1 To prepare the egg shell, pierce a hole in each end and blow out the contents into a bowl. Using a small pastry nozzle or skewer, enlarge the hole in one end, wash out the shell and leave to dry completely. Leave in a warm oven which has been turned off, or dry gently with a hair dryer; the shells must be completely dry before filling.

2 Cover the smaller hole with tape and place in an egg carton. Fill a paper cone with melted chocolate. Insert the tip into the egg and slowly force chocolate into the shell, pulling the tip out as the egg is filled. Leave to set overnight.

3 To take the shell from the chocolate, gently crack and peel off. Avoid touching the eggs with fingers as they leave prints. If shells are difficult to remove, freeze eggs for 1 hour and try again. Wrap each egg in coloured foil or tie with ribbon.

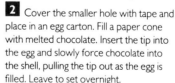

Quick Chocolate Curls

Chocolate curls make an ideal decoration for many desserts and cakes, whether these are made from chocolate or other flavours. These curls can be made very quickly using a vegetable peeler, and can be stored for several weeks in an airtight container.

1 Bring a thick piece or bar of chocolate to room temperature (chocolate that is too cold will 'grate' and too warm will slice). With a swivel-bladed peeler held over a plate or baking sheet, pull the blade firmly along the edge of the chocolate and allow curls to fall on to the plate or baking sheet in a single layer.

2 Use a skewer or toothpick to transfer curls to the dessert or cake, as fingers will melt the curls.

Chunky Chocolate Curls

These curls are best made with dark chocolate which is melted with vegetable fat (about 5 g/1 teaspoon per 30 g/1 oz of chocolate), which keeps the chocolate from hardening completely.

1 Melt 170 g/6 oz bittersweet or semi-sweet chocolate with 30 g/2 tbsp pure white vegetable fat, stirring until smooth. Pour into a small rectangular or square tin lined with foil or non-stick baking paper to produce a block about 2.5 cm/1 in thick. Refrigerate until set.

2 Allow the block to come to room temperature, remove from the tin, then use a swivel-bladed peeler to produce short chunky curls, or grate as desired.

Chocolate Scrolls or Short Round Curls

Temper dark or white chocolate, or use chocolate prepared for Chunky Chocolate Curls to produce these scrolls.

1 Pour prepared chocolate on to a marble slab or the back of a baking sheet. Using a metal palette knife, spread to about 3 mm/⅛ in thick and allow to set until just firm, about 30 minutes.

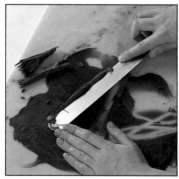

2 To make long scrolls, use the blade of a long, sharp knife on the surface of the chocolate and, with both hands, push away from your body at a 25–45° angle to scrape off a thin layer of chocolate. Twist the handle of the knife about a quarter of a circle to make a slightly wider scroll. To make shorter 'cup-shaped' curls, use a teaspoon to scrape the chocolate away.

3 A variety of shapes and sizes can be produced, depending on the temperature of the chocolate and the tool used to scrape the chocolate. Metal palette knives, paint scrapers, tablespoons and even a wide, straight pastry scraper can be used. The colder the chocolate, the more it will splinter; warm chocolate will give a softer, looser curl, but do not allow chocolate to become too soft or warm or it will be difficult to handle and may bloom.

Chocolate Shapes

These are easy to prepare with melted chocolate, and are ideal for decorating gâteaux or desserts.

1 Prepare melted chocolate and pour on to a non-stick baking paper-lined baking sheet and spread evenly to a thickness of about 3 mm/⅛ in. Allow to cool for 30 minutes or until firm. Invert the chocolate on to another sheet of non-stick baking paper and, using a sharp knife and straight edge, trim the edges to make a perfect rectangle.

2 Using the straight edge, mark even squares, rectangles or diamond shapes and cut with a knife.

3 Alternatively, use small metal biscuit or aspic cutters to make decorative shapes.

4 Use a plain piping tip to punch a hole in the top and thread with a ribbon for chocolate ornaments, then use a contrasting chocolate to decorate with designs or names.

Chocolate Drizzles

You can have great fun making random shapes or, with a steady hand, special designs.

1 Melt chocolate and pour into a paper cone or small icing bag fitted with a very small plain nozzle. Drizzle on to a non-stick baking paper-lined baking sheet in small, self-contained lattice shapes, such as circles or squares. Allow to set until firm (about 30 minutes) before carefully peeling off paper.

2 Chocolate can be used in many designs such as flowers or butterflies. Use non-stick baking paper as tracing paper and pipe chocolate over the chosen design or shape as a guide.

3 For butterflies, pipe chocolate on to individually cut squares and leave until just beginning to set. Use a long, thin box (such as an egg carton) and place the butterfly shape in the box or between the cups so it is bent in the centre, creating the butterfly shape. Chill until needed.

Chocolate Leaves

You can use any fresh, non-toxic leaf with distinct veins such as rose, bay or lemon leaves.

1 Wash and dry leaves thoroughly. Melt the chocolate and use a pastry brush or spoon to coat the veined side of each leaf completely.

2 Place coated leaves chocolate-side up on a non-stick baking paper-lined baking sheet to set.

3 Starting at the stem end, gently peel away the leaf. Store the chocolate leaves in a cool place until needed.

Making a Paper Cone

A paper cone is ideal for piping small amounts of messy liquids like chocolate as it is small, easy to handle and disposable, avoiding the cleaning of an icing bag.

Chocolate Cups

Large or small cup-liners or sweet cases can be used to make cases to fill with ice creams, mousses or liqueurs. Use double liners inside each other for extra support.

1 Melt the chocolate and, using a spoon or pastry brush, completely coat the bottom and side of the case. Allow to set, then repeat for a second layer. Allow to set for several hours or overnight.

2 Carefully peel off the cup-liner or sweet case, set on a baking sheet and fill as desired.

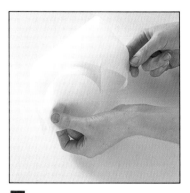

1 Fold a square of non-stick baking paper in half to form a triangle. With the triangle point facing you, fold the left corner down to the centre.

2 Fold the right corner down and wrap completely around folded left corner, forming a cone. Fold the ends into the cone. Spoon the melted chocolate or liquid into the cone and fold the top edges over to enclose the filling.

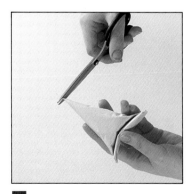

3 When ready to pipe, snip off the end of the point to make a hole about 3 mm/ ⅛ in diameter. Use to pipe chocolates, white icings and melted preserves.

4 Another method is to use a small heavy-duty freezer or plastic bag. Place a piping tip in one corner. Fill as above, squeezing the filling into one corner and twisting the top to seal. Snip off the corner of the bag and squeeze gently to pipe the design.

Chocolate Layer Cake

The cake layers can be made ahead, wrapped and frozen for future use. Always defrost cakes completely before icing.

Serves 10–12

INGREDIENTS
unsweetened cocoa for dusting
225 g/8 oz can cooked whole
    beetroot, drained and juice
    reserved
115 g/4 oz/½ cup unsalted butter,
    softened
550 g/19¾ oz/2½ cups (packed) light
    brown sugar
3 eggs
15 ml/1 tbsp vanilla essence
85 g/3 oz unsweetened chocolate,
    melted
285 g/10 oz/2 cups plain flour
10 ml/2 tsp baking powder
2.5 ml/½ tsp salt
125 ml/4 fl oz/½ cup buttermilk
chocolate curls (optional)

CHOCOLATE GANACHE FROSTING
450 ml/16 fl oz/2 cups whipping or
    double cream
500 g/1 lb 2 oz fine quality,
    bittersweet or semi-sweet
    chocolate, chopped
15 ml/1 tbsp vanilla essence

bittersweet chocolate

unsweetened chocolate

eggs

vanilla essence

beetroot

1 Preheat oven to 180°C/350°F/Gas 4. Grease two 23 cm/9 in cake tins and dust bottom and sides with cocoa. Grate beetroot and add to beet juice. With electric mixer, beat the butter, brown sugar, eggs and vanilla until pale and fluffy (3–5 minutes). Reduce speed and beat in chocolate.

2 In a bowl, sift flour, baking powder and salt. With mixer on low speed and beginning and ending with flour mixture, alternately beat in flour mixture in fourths and buttermilk in thirds. Add beets and juice and beat for 1 minute. Divide between tins and bake for 30–35 minutes or until a cake tester inserted in the centre comes out clean. Cool for 10 minutes, then unmould and cool completely.

3 To make the frosting, in a heavy-based saucepan over medium heat, heat cream until it just begins to boil, stirring occasionally to prevent it scorching. Remove from heat and stir in chocolate, stirring constantly until melted and smooth. Stir in vanilla. Strain into a bowl and refrigerate, stirring every 10 minutes, until spreadable, about 1 hour.

4 Assemble the cake. Place one layer on a serving plate and spread with one-third of the ganache. Turn cake layer bottom side up and spread remaining ganache over top and side of cake. If using, top with the chocolate curls. Allow ganache to set for 20–30 minutes, then refrigerate before serving.

Chocolate Mint-filled Cupcakes

For extra mint flavour, chop 8 thin mint cream-filled after dinner mints and fold into the cake batter before filling paper liners. Omit the cream filling if you wish.

Makes 12

INGREDIENTS

240 g/8 oz/2 cups plain flour
5 ml/1 tsp bicarbonate of soda
pinch of salt
55 g/2 oz/½ cup unsweetened cocoa
140 g/5 oz/10 tbsp unsalted butter, softened
300 g/10½ oz/1½ cups caster sugar
3 eggs
5 ml/1 tsp peppermint essence
250 ml/8 fl oz/1 cup milk

MINT CREAM FILLING

300 ml/10 fl oz/1¼ cups double or whipping cream
5 ml/1 tsp peppermint essence

CHOCOLATE MINT GLAZE

170 g/6 oz plain chocolate
115 g/4 oz/½ cup unsalted butter
5 ml/1 tsp peppermint essence

plain chocolate

eggs

cocoa

peppermint essence

1 Preheat oven to 180°C/350°F/Gas 4. Line a 12 × 6.5 cm/2½ in bun tray with paper cases. Into a bowl, sift together flour, bicarbonate of soda, salt and cocoa. In a large mixing bowl with electric mixer, beat butter and sugar until light and creamy, about 3–5 minutes. Add eggs one at a time, beating well after each addition; beat in peppermint essence. On low speed, beat in flour-cocoa mixture alternately with milk, until just blended. Spoon into paper cases.

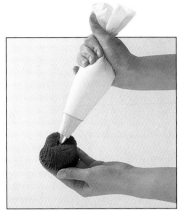

2 Bake for 12–15 minutes until cake tester inserted in centre comes out clean: do not over-bake. Immediately remove cupcakes to wire rack to cool completely. When cool, remove paper cases. Prepare filling. In a small bowl with electric mixer, whip the cream and peppermint essence until stiff peaks form. Spoon into a small icing bag fitted with a small plain tip. Push tip into the bottom of a cupcake and squeeze gently releasing about 15 ml/1 tbsp of cream into centre. Repeat with remaining cupcakes.

3 Prepare glaze. In a saucepan over low heat, melt chocolate and butter, stirring until smooth. Remove from heat and stir in peppermint essence. Cool, then spread on top of each cake.

Chocolate Chestnut Roulade

For an alternative decoration, dip 12 glacéed chestnuts halfway into melted plain chocolate, allow to set and use to decorate the roulade.

Serves 10–12

INGREDIENTS

170 g/6 oz bittersweet chocolate, chopped
30 ml/2 tbsp unsweetened cocoa, sifted
65 ml/2 fl oz/¼ cup strong coffee or espresso
6 eggs, separated
pinch of cream of tartar
85 g/3 oz/6 tbsp caster sugar
5 ml/1 tsp vanilla essence
unsweetened cocoa for dusting
glacéed chestnuts to decorate

CHESTNUT CREAM FILLING

450 ml/16 fl oz/2 cups double cream
30 ml/1 fl oz/2 tbsp rum or coffee-flavour liqueur
350 g/12 oz/1½ cups canned sweetened chestnut purée
115 g/4 oz bittersweet chocolate, grated

chestnut purée

bittersweet chocolate

coffee

coffee-flavour liqueur

glacéed chestnuts

1 Preheat oven to 180°C/350°F/Gas 4. Grease bottom and sides of 39 × 27 × 2.5 cm/15½ × 10½ × 1 in Swiss roll tin. Line bottom with non-stick baking paper, allowing 2.5 cm/1 in overhang. In the top of a double boiler, over low heat, melt the chocolate, stirring frequently until smooth. Set aside. Dissolve the cocoa with the coffee to make a smooth paste. Set aside.

4 Prepare filling. In a medium bowl with electric mixer, whip the cream and rum or liqueur until soft peaks form. Beat a spoonful of cream into the chestnut purée to lighten it, then fold in the remaining cream and grated chocolate. Reserve a quarter of chestnut cream mixture for garnish.

2 In a mixing bowl with electric mixer, beat egg yolks with half the sugar until pale and thick, about 3–5 minutes. Slowly beat in the melted chocolate and cocoa-coffee paste until just blended.

In a bowl with electric mixer, beat egg whites and cream of tartar until stiff peaks form. Sprinkle sugar over whites in two batches and beat until whites are stiff and glossy; beat in vanilla. Stir a spoonful of whites into chocolate mixture to lighten it, then fold in remaining whites. Spoon into tin. Bake for 20–25 minutes or until cake springs back when touched with a fingertip.

COOK'S TIP

Beating egg whites should always be the last step in preparation of cakes or any other recipes. Once they are beaten, they should be folded in immediately and never held.

3 Meanwhile, dust a dish towel with cocoa. When cake is done, turn out on to towel immediately and remove paper. Starting at a narrow end, roll cake and towel together Swiss roll fashion. Cool completely.

5 Assemble the roulade. Unroll roulade and, if you like, trim edges. Spread chestnut cream mixture to within 2.5 cm/1 in of edge of the cake. Using the towel to lift the cake, gently roll cake Swiss roll fashion.

6 Place roulade seam-side down on a serving plate. Spread the reserved chestnut cream over the top of the roulade, and spoon some into small icing bag fitted with a medium star tip. Pipe rosettes down the sides of roulade and decorate with glacéed chestnuts.

Marbled Chocolate-Peanut Butter Cake

This cake cannot be tested with a cake tester because the peanut butter remains soft in the centre. Rely on the fingertip method: the cake should spring back when touched after 50–60 minutes.

Serves 12–14

INGREDIENTS
115 g/4 oz unsweetened chocolate,
    chopped
225 g/8 oz/1 cup unsalted butter,
    softened
225 g/8 oz/1 cup smooth or chunky
    peanut butter
200 g/6½ oz/1 cup granulated sugar
220 g/7 oz/1 cup (packed) light
    brown sugar
5 eggs
285 g/10 oz/2 cups plain flour
10 ml/2 tsp baking powder
2.5 ml/½ tsp salt
125 ml/4 fl oz/½ cup milk
55 g/2 oz/⅓ cup chocolate chips

CHOCOLATE PEANUT BUTTER GLAZE
30 g/1 oz/2 tbsp butter, cut up
30 g/1 oz/2 tbsp smooth peanut butter
45 ml/3 tbsp golden syrup
5 ml/1 tsp vanilla essence
170 g/6 oz plain chocolate, broken
    into pieces

peanut butter

unsweetened chocolate

chocolate chips

brown sugar

1 Preheat oven to 180°C/350°F/Gas 4. Generously grease and flour a 3 litre/5 pint/12 cup tube or ring mould. In the top of a double boiler over low heat, melt the chocolate.

4 Pour half the batter into another bowl. Stir the melted chocolate into one half of the batter until well blended. Stir the chocolate chips into the other half of the batter.

2 In a large mixing bowl with electric mixer, beat butter, peanut butter and sugars until light and creamy, about 3–5 minutes, scraping side of bowl occasionally. Add eggs one at a time, beating well after each addition.

5 Using a large spoon, drop alternate spoonfuls of chocolate batter and peanut butter batter into the prepared tin. Using a knife, pull through the batters to create a swirled marbled effect; do not let the knife touch side or bottom of tin and do not over-mix. Bake the cake for 50–60 minutes until top of cake springs back when touched with a fingertip. Cool cake in the tin on wire rack for 10 minutes. Unmould on to rack to cool completely.

3 In a medium bowl, stir together flour, baking powder and salt. Add to the butter mixture alternately with the milk until just blended.

6 Prepare glaze. Combine all the ingredients and 15 ml/1 tbsp water in a small saucepan. Melt over low heat, stirring until well blended and smooth. Cool slightly. When slightly thickened, drizzle the glaze over the cake allowing it to run the down side.

Chocolate Pecan Torte

This torte uses finely ground nuts instead of flour.
Toast then cool the nuts before grinding finely in a
food processor. Do not over-grind the nuts, as the oils
will form a paste.

Serves 16

INGREDIENTS

200 g/7 oz bittersweet or plain
    chocolate, chopped
140 g/5 oz/10 tbsp unsalted butter,
    cut into pieces
4 eggs
100 g/3½ oz/½ cup caster sugar
10 ml/2 tsp vanilla essence
115 g/4 oz/1 cup ground pecans
10 ml/2 tsp ground cinnamon
24 toasted pecan halves to decorate
    (optional)

CHOCOLATE HONEY GLAZE

115 g/4 oz bittersweet or semi-sweet
    chocolate, chopped
60 g/2 oz/¼ cup unsalted butter, cut
    into pieces
30 ml/2 tbsp honey
pinch of ground cinnamon

plain chocolate

vanilla essence

eggs

honey

cinnamon

pecans

1 Preheat oven to 180°C/350°F/Gas 4.
Grease a 20 × 5 cm/8 × 2½ in
springform tin; line with baking paper
then grease the paper. Wrap bottom and
side of tin with foil to prevent water
seeping in. In a saucepan over a low heat,
melt chocolate and butter, stirring until
smooth. Remove from heat. In a mixing
bowl with electric mixer, beat eggs, sugar
and vanilla until frothy, 1–2 minutes. Stir in
melted chocolate, ground nuts and
cinnamon. Pour into tin..

2 Place foil-wrapped tin in a large
roasting tin and pour boiling water into
roasting tin, to come 2 cm/¾ in up the
side of the springform tin. Bake for 25–30
minutes until edge of cake is set, but
centre is soft. Remove from water bath
and remove foil. Cool on rack.

3 Prepare glaze. In a small saucepan
over low heat, melt chocolate, butter,
honey and cinnamon, stirring until
smooth; remove from heat. Carefully dip
toasted pecan halves halfway into glaze
and place on a non-stick baking paper-
lined baking sheet until set. The glaze will
have thickened slightly.

4 Remove side from springform tin and
invert cake on to wire rack. Remove the
tin bottom and paper, so bottom of cake
is now the top. Pour thickened glaze over
cake, tilting rack slightly to spread glaze.
Use a metal palette knife to smooth sides.
Arrange nuts around outside edge of
torte and allow glaze to set.

French Chocolate Cake

This very dense chocolate cake can be made up to 3 days before serving, but decorate with icing sugar on the day it is to be served.

Serves 10

INGREDIENTS
250 g/9 oz bittersweet chocolate, chopped
225 g/8 oz/1 cup unsalted butter, cut into pieces
100 g/3½ oz/½ cup granulated sugar
30 ml/2 tbsp brandy or orange-flavour liqueur
5 eggs
15 ml/1 tbsp plain flour
icing sugar for dusting
whipped or soured cream for serving

bittersweet chocolate

eggs

brandy

1 Preheat oven to 180°C/350°F/Gas 4. Generously grease a 23 × 5 cm/9 × 2 in springform tin. Line bottom with non-stick baking paper and grease the paper. Wrap bottom and side of tin in foil to prevent water seeping into cake. In a saucepan over a low heat, melt chocolate, butter and sugar, stirring frequently until smooth; cool slightly. Stir in the liqueur. In a large mixing bowl with electric mixer, beat eggs lightly, about 1 minute. Beat in flour then slowly beat in the chocolate mixture until well blended. Pour into tin.

2 Place filled, foil-wrapped tin in a large roasting tin and pour boiling water into roasting tin, to come 2 cm/¾ in up the side of the springform tin. Bake for 25–30 minutes until edge of cake is set, but centre is still soft. Remove tin from water bath and remove foil. Cool on wire rack completely (cake will sink in the centre and may crack).

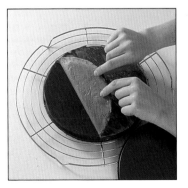

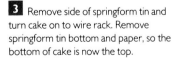

3 Remove side of springform tin and turn cake on to wire rack. Remove springform tin bottom and paper, so the bottom of cake is now the top.

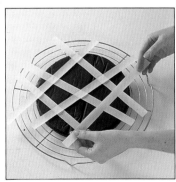

4 Cut 6–8 strips of non-stick baking paper 2.5 cm/1 in wide and place randomly over cake or make a lattice-style pattern if you wish. Dust cake with icing sugar; then carefully remove paper. Slide cake on to a serving plate and serve with cream.

White Chocolate Mousse and Strawberry Layer Cake

The strawberries used in this cake can be replaced by raspberries or blackberries and the appropriate flavour liqueur.

Serves 10

INGREDIENTS
115 g/4 oz fine quality white chocolate, chopped
125 ml/4 fl oz/½ cup whipping or double cream
125 ml/4 fl oz/½ cup milk
15 ml/1 tbsp rum or vanilla essence
115 g/4 oz/8 tbsp unsalted butter, softened
175 g/6 oz/¾ cup granulated sugar
3 eggs
285 g/10 oz/2 cups plain flour
5 ml/1 tsp baking powder
pinch of salt
675 g/1½ lb fresh strawberries, sliced, plus extra for decoration
750 ml/1¼ pints/3 cups whipping cream
30 ml/2 tbsp rum or strawberry-flavour liqueur

WHITE CHOCOLATE MOUSSE FILLING
250 g/9 oz fine quality white chocolate, chopped
350 ml/12 fl oz/1½ cups whipping or double cream
30 ml/2 tbsp rum or strawberry-flavour liqueur

strawberries

white chocolate

1 Preheat oven to 180°C/350°F/Gas 4. Grease and flour two 23 × 5 cm/9 × 2 in cake tins. Line the base of the tins with non-stick baking paper. Melt chocolate and cream in a double boiler over a low heat, stirring until smooth. Stir in milk and rum or vanilla essence; set aside to cool.

4 Prepare mousse. In medium saucepan over low heat, melt chocolate and cream until smooth, stirring frequently. Stir in rum or strawberry-flavour liqueur and pour into a bowl. Refrigerate until mixture is just set. With a wire whisk, whip lightly until mixture has a 'mousse' consistency.

2 In a large mixing bowl with electric mixer, beat the butter and sugar until light and creamy, about 3–5 minutes, scraping sides of bowl occasionally. Add eggs one at a time, beating well after each addition. In a small bowl, stir together flour, baking powder and salt. Alternately add flour and melted chocolate to eggs in batches, just until blended. Pour batter into tins and spread evenly.

5 Assemble cake. With serrated knife, slice both cake layers in half crosswise, making four layers. Place one layer on plate and spread one third of mousse on top. Arrange about one third of sliced strawberries over mousse. Place second layer on top and spread with another third of mousse. Arrange another third of sliced strawberries over mousse. Place third layer on top and spread with remaining mousse and cover with remaining sliced strawberries. Cover with last cake layer.

3 Bake for 20–25 minutes until cake tester inserted in centre comes out clea Cool on wire rack for 10 minutes. Turn cakes out on to wire rack, peel off pape and cool completely.

6 Whip the cream with the rum or liqueur until firm peaks form. Spread about half the whipped cream over top and sides of cake. Spoon remaining cream into a decorating bag fitted with a medium star tip and pipe scrolls on top of cake. Garnish with remaining strawberries.

Luxury White Chocolate Cheesecake

To ensure an even crust, use a dessertspoon or tablespoon to press crumbs to bottom and side of tin.

Serves 16–20

INGREDIENTS

140 g/5 oz (about 16–18) digestive
   biscuits
70 g/2½ oz/½ cup blanched
   hazelnuts, toasted
55 g/2 oz/4 tbsp unsalted butter,
   melted
2.5 ml/½ tsp ground cinnamon

FILLING

350 g/12 oz fine quality white
   chocolate, chopped
125 ml/4 fl oz/½ cup whipping or
   double cream
675 g/1½ lb/3 × 8 oz packets cream
   cheese, softened
55 g/2 oz/⅓ cup granulated sugar
4 eggs
30 ml/2 tbsp hazelnut-flavour liqueur
   or 15 ml/1 tbsp vanilla essence

TOPPING

425 ml/15 fl oz/1¾ cup soured cream
55 g/2 oz/¼ cup granulated sugar
15 ml/1 tbsp hazelnut-flavour liqueur
   or 5 ml/1 tsp vanilla essence
white chocolate curls to decorate
cocoa for dusting (optional)

digestive biscuits

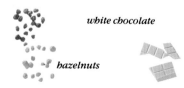

white chocolate

hazelnuts

1 Preheat oven to 180°C/350°F/Gas 4. Lightly grease a 23 × 7.5 cm/9 × 3 in springform tin. In a food processor with metal blade, process biscuits and hazelnuts until fine crumbs form. Pour in butter and cinnamon. Process just until blended. Using the back of a spoon, press on to bottom and to within 1 cm/½ in of top of side of pan. Bake for 5–7 minutes, until just set. Remove to rack to cool. Lower oven temperature to 150°C/300°F/Gas 3.

2 Prepare filling. In a small saucepan over a low heat, melt the white chocolate and cream until smooth, stirring frequently. Set aside to cool.

4 Prepare topping. In a small bowl whisk the soured cream, sugar and liqueur or vanilla. Pour over cheesecake, spreading evenly, and return to oven. Bake for a further 5–7 minutes. Turn off oven, but do not open door for 1 hour.

3 In a large bowl with an electric mixer, beat the cream cheese and sugar until smooth, about 2–4 minutes. Add eggs one at a time, beating well after each addition, scraping bowl occasionally. Slowly beat in the white chocolate mixture and liqueur or vanilla essence.

Pour into baked crust. Place tin on baking sheet. Bake for 45–55 minutes, or until edge of cake is firm but centre is still slightly soft, do not allow to brown. Remove to wire rack while preparing topping. Increase oven temperature to 200°C/400°F/Gas 6.

5 Remove to wire rack to cool to room temperature. Run sharp knife around edge of cake in tin to separate it from side; this helps prevent cracking. Cool completely then refrigerate, loosely covered, overnight.

6 To serve, run sharp knife around edge of tin to loosen cake. Remove side of springform tin. If you like, slide sharp knife under crust to separate cake from bottom and with metal palette knife, slide carefully on to serving plate. Alternatively, leave cake on tin bottom to avoid breaking crust or surface and serve from bottom of tin. Decorate top of cake with chocolate curls and dust lightly with cocoa.

Mississippi Mud Cake

There are many versions of this cake, but all of them are based on a dark cocoa-based chocolate cake, which is meant to be reminiscent of the cocoa-black shores of the Mississippi River.

Serves 8–10

INGREDIENTS
unsweetened cocoa for dusting
285 g/10 oz/2 cups plain flour
5 ml/1 tsp baking powder
140 g/5 oz unsweetened chocolate
225 g/8 oz/1 cup unsalted butter
300 ml/10 fl oz/1¼ cups strong coffee
    or espresso
pinch of salt
400 g/14 oz/2 cups granulated sugar
60 ml/2 fl oz/¼ cup bourbon or
    whisky
2 eggs, lightly beaten
10 ml/2 tsp vanilla essence
130 g/4½ oz/1 cup sweetened
    desiccated coconut
350 ml/12 fl oz/1½ cups whipping or
    double cream
5 ml/1 tsp vanilla essence
Coconut Ruffles (see step 6)

FILLING
250 ml/8 oz/1 cup evaporated milk
115 g/4 oz/½ cup (packed) light
    brown sugar
115 g/4 oz/8 tbsp unsalted butter
85 g/3 oz plain chocolate
3 egg yolks, lightly beaten
5 ml/1 tsp vanilla essence
225 g/8 oz/2 cups pecans, chopped
70 g/2½ oz/1 cup miniature
    marshmallows

plain chocolate

unsweetened chocolate

eggs

pecans

miniature marshmallows

desiccated coconut

1 Preheat the oven to 180°C/350°F/ Gas 4. Grease 2 × 23 cm/9 in cake tins, dust bottoms and sides with cocoa. In a bowl sift flour and baking powder. In a saucepan over low heat, melt chocolate, butter, coffee, salt and sugar, stirring occasionally until smooth and sugar dissolved. Stir in bourbon or whisky. Pour chocolate mixture into a bowl and cool slightly. With an electric mixer on medium speed, beat in eggs and vanilla, decrease speed and beat in the flour; stir in coconut. Pour into prepared tins.

2 Bake for 25–30 minutes until cake tester inserted in centre comes out with just a few crumbs attached; do not over-bake or the cake will be too dry. Cool on wire rack for 10 minutes. Remove cakes from the tins and place on a wire rack to cool completely.

3 For the filling, combine the evaporated milk, sugar, butter, chocolate, egg yolks and vanilla in a large heavy-based saucepan. Cook over medium heat, stirring frequently for 8–10 minutes until chocolate is melted and smooth and mixture is thick enough to coat the back of a wooden spoon; do not boil or mixture will curdle. Remove from heat and stir in nuts and marshmallows, stirring until melted. Refrigerate until thick enough to spread, stirring occasionally to prevent a skin forming.

4 Assemble cake. With serrated knife, slice both cake layers in half crosswise, making four layers. Spread each of the bottom cake layers with half the chocolate nut filling and cover each bottom half with its respective top layer.

5 In a medium bowl, whip the cream and the vanilla until firm peaks form. Place one filled cake layer on a cake plate and spread with half the whipped cream. Top with the second filled cake layer and spread with the remaining cream, swirling cream to form an attractive pattern.

6 Make the Coconut Ruffles. Using a heavy hammer and nail, puncture the eyes of a fresh coconut. Drain off the liquid and reserve if wished. Place coconut in a strong plastic bag and hit shell very hard with the hammer to crack coconut open. With a strong blunt-bladed knife, separate the flesh from the shell; it will break into medium sized pieces. Rinse pieces under cold running water and store in cold water. With a swivel-bladed peeler, draw the blade along the curved edge of a coconut piece to make thin wide curls with a brown edge.

Chocolate Cappuccino Cake

If desired the cake can be left whole and rolled roulade-style, or baked in 2 × 23 cm/9 in tins for a round cake.

Serves 8–10

INGREDIENTS
170 g/6 oz plain chocolate, chopped
10 ml/2 tsp instant espresso powder (or 15 ml/1 tbsp instant coffee powder) dissolved in 45 ml/3 tbsp boiling water
6 eggs, separated
140 g/5 oz/¾ cup granulated sugar
pinch of cream of tartar
unsweetened cocoa for sifting
chocolate coffee beans to decorate

COFFEE CREAM FILLING
175 ml/6 fl oz/¾ cup whipping or double cream
30 g/1 oz/2 tbsp granulated sugar
225 g/8 oz mascarpone or cream cheese, softened
30 ml/2 tbsp coffee-flavour liqueur
30 g/1 oz plain chocolate, grated

COFFEE BUTTERCREAM
4 egg yolks, at room temperature
70 ml/2½ fl oz/⅓ cup light golden syrup
55 g/2 oz/⅓ cup granulated sugar
225 g/8 oz/1 cup unsalted butter, cut into small pieces and softened
15 ml/1 tbsp instant espresso powder dissolved in 5–10 ml/1–2 tsp boiling water
15–30 ml/1–2 tbsp coffee-flavour liqueur

cocoa

plain chocolate

instant coffee powder

eggs

chocolate coffee beans

1 Preheat oven to 180°C/350°F/Gas 4. Grease a 40 × 20.7 cm/15½ × 10½ in baking sheet. Line with non-stick baking paper, leaving a 5 cm/2 in overhang on each narrow end. Grease the paper. In the top of a double boiler, over low heat, heat chocolate and dissolved coffee powder until melted and smooth, stirring frequently. Set aside. In a bowl with an electric mixer, beat egg yolks and sugar until thick and light-coloured, 3–5 minutes. Reduce speed to low and beat in chocolate mixture until blended.

2 In a large bowl with electric mixer with cleaned beaters, beat the egg whites and cream of tartar until stiff peaks begin to form. Do not overbeat. Stir a spoonful of whites into the chocolate mixture to lighten it, then fold in remaining whites. Pour batter into the prepared tin, spreading into corners and smoothing the top evenly. Bake for 12–15 minutes until top springs back when touched lightly with a fingertip. Sprinkle clean dish towel with cocoa to cover and turn cake out on to towel. Peel off paper and cool.

3 Prepare filling. In a medium bowl with an electric mixer, whip the cream and sugar until soft peaks form. In another bowl, beat the mascarpone or cream cheese and liqueur until light and smooth. Stir in the grated chocolate and fold in the whipped cream. Cover and refrigerate until ready for use.

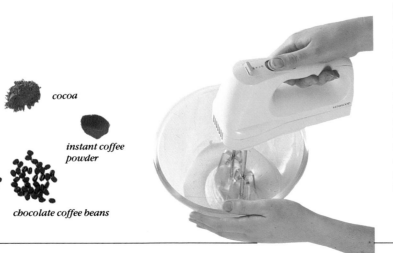

4 Prepare buttercream. In a bowl with an electric mixer on high speed, beat yolks until thick and pale-coloured, 5–6 minutes. In a saucepan over medium heat, cook syrup and sugar until mixture boils, stirring constantly. With mixer on medium-low speed, slowly pour hot syrup over beaten yolks in a slow stream. Continue beating until mixture feels cool, 5–6 minutes. Beat in butter a few pieces at a time until mixture is smooth. Beat in dissolved coffee and liqueur. Refrigerate until ready to use, but bring to room temperature before spreading.

5 Assemble cake. With a serrated knife, trim off any crisp edges of cake. Cut cake crosswise into three equal strips. Place one cake strip on a cake plate and spread with half the coffee cream filling. Cover with a second cake strip and the remaining filling. Top with the remaining cake strip.

6 Spoon about one third coffee buttercream into a small decorating bag fitted with a small star tip. Spread remaining buttercream on top and sides of cake. Pipe lattice or scroll design on top of cake and around edges of cake and decorate with chocolate coffee beans. Refrigerate cake if not serving immediately, but allow to stand at room temperature 30 minutes before serving.

Chocolate Pine Nut Tart

Lemon zest could be used instead of orange and a combination of white and plain chocolate substituted for all plain.

Serves 8

INGREDIENTS
215 g/7½ oz/1½ cups plain flour
50 g/1¾ oz/¼ cup caster sugar
pinch of salt
grated zest of ½ orange
115 g/4 oz/½ cup unsalted butter, cut
    into small pieces
3 egg yolks, lightly beaten
15–30 ml/1–2 tbsp iced water

FILLING
2 eggs
45 g/1½ oz/3 tbsp caster sugar
grated zest of 1 orange
15 ml/1 tbsp orange-flavour liqueur
250 ml/8 fl oz/1 cup whipping cream
115 g/4 oz plain chocolate, chopped
85 g/3 oz/¾ cup pine nuts, toasted

TO DECORATE
1 orange
50 g/1¾ oz/¼ cup granulated sugar
125 ml/4 fl oz/½ cup water

1 In a food processor with metal blade, process flour, sugar, salt and orange zest to blend. Add butter and process for 20–30 seconds until mixture resembles coarse crumbs. Add yolks and using pulse-action process until dough begins to stick together; do not allow dough to form a ball or pastry will be tough. If dough appears dry, add 1–2 tbsp iced water, little by little, just until dough holds together. Turn dough on to lightly floured surface and knead gently until blended. Shape into flat disc and wrap in non-stick baking paper or clear film. Refrigerate for 2–3 hours or overnight.

orange

eggs

pine nuts

plain chocolate

2 Lightly butter a 23 cm/9 in tart tin with removable bottom. Soften dough for 5–10 minutes at room temperature. On a well-floured surface, roll out dough into a 28 cm/11 in round, about 3 mm/⅛ in thick. Roll dough loosely around rolling pin and unroll over tart tin. Ease dough into tin. With floured fingers, press overhang down slightly towards centre (making top edge thicker).

3 Roll a rolling pin over edge to cut off excess dough. Now press thicker top edge against side of tin to form rim slightly higher than tin. Prick bottom with fork. Refrigerate for 1 hour. Preheat oven to 200°C/400°F/Gas 6. Line tart shell with foil or non-stick baking paper; fill with dry beans or rice. Bake for 5 minutes, then lift out foil with beans and bake 5 more minutes, until set. Remove to wire rack to cool slightly. Lower temperature to 180°C/350°F/Gas 4.

4 Prepare filling. In a medium bowl beat the eggs, sugar, zest and liqueur. Blend in the cream. Sprinkle the chocolate evenly over bottom of tart shell, then sprinkle over pine nuts. Place tin on baking sheet and gently pour egg and cream mixture into tart shell. Bake tart for 20–30 minutes, until pastry is golden and custard is set. Remove to wire rack to cool slightly.

5 Prepare decoration. With vegetable peeler, remove thin strips of orange zest and cut into julienne strips. In a small saucepan over high heat, bring julienne strips, sugar and water to the boil. Boil for 5–8 minutes until syrup is thickened; then stir in 1 tbsp cold water to stop cooking.

6 With a pastry brush, carefully glaze tart with the orange-sugar syrup and arrange julienne orange strips over tart. Remove side of tart tin and slide tart on to plate. Serve warm.

COOK'S TIP
If you do not wish to prepare the garnish, simply heat 30 ml/2 tbsp marmalade and 5 ml/1 tsp water until dissolved. Brush over the surface of the warm tart.

Chocolate Chip Pecan Pie

Bittersweet chocolate can be substituted for unsweetened chocolate, but use only 100 g/3½ oz/½ cup brown sugar and 125 ml/4 fl oz/½ cup syrup or the tart will be too sweet.

Serves 8–10

INGREDIENTS
180 g/6¼ oz/1¼ cups plain flour
15 ml/1 tbsp caster sugar
2.5 ml/½ tsp salt
115 g/4 oz/½ cup unsalted butter, cut
   into small pieces
125 ml/4 fl oz/½ cup iced water

FILLING
85 g/3 oz unsweetened chocolate,
   chopped
55 g/2 oz/4 tbsp butter, cut into
   pieces
3 eggs
165 g/5½ oz/¾ cup (packed) light
   brown sugar
175 ml/6 fl oz/¾ cup corn or glucose
   syrup
15 ml/1 tbsp vanilla essence
225 g/8 oz/2 cups pecan halves
85 g/3 oz/½ cup plain chocolate chips

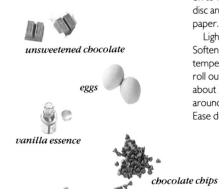
unsweetened chocolate

eggs

vanilla essence

chocolate chips

pecans

1 Prepare pastry. In a food processor fitted with a metal blade, process flour, sugar and salt to blend. Add butter and process for 15–20 seconds until mixture resembles coarse crumbs. With machine running, add iced water through feed tube, just until dough begins to stick together; do not allow dough to form a ball or pastry will be tough. Turn dough on to floured work surface, shape into flat disc and wrap tightly in non-stick baking paper. Refrigerate for 1 hour.

   Lightly butter a 23 cm/9 in tart tin. Soften dough for 10–15 minutes at room temperature. On a well-floured surface, roll out dough into a 30 cm/12 in round, about 3 mm/⅛ in thick. Roll dough loosely around rolling pin and unroll over tart tin. Ease dough into plate.

2 With kitchen scissors, trim the pastry even with the rim of the tin; using fingers, flatten to rim of tin. Re-roll trimmings to a long rectangle and, with a sharp knife, cut thin strips about 5 mm/¼ in wide. Plait three strips together. Repeat until you have sufficient plaits to fit around the pie edge. Brush pastry edge with water and press pastry plaits to edge. Prick bottom of dough with fork. Refrigerate for 30 minutes.

3 Preheat oven to 200°C/400°F/Gas 6. Line pastry shell with foil or non-stick baking paper; fill with dry beans or rice. Bake for 5 minutes, carefully lift out foil with beans and bake for 5 more minutes. Remove to wire rack to cool slightly. Lower oven temperature to 190°C/375°F/Gas 5.

4 Prepare filling. In a small saucepan over low heat, melt the chocolate and butter, stirring until smooth. Set aside to cool slightly.

COOK'S TIP

This pie can also be made in a tart tin with a removable bottom. Try to arrange the pecans in concentric circles for a more sophisticated looking tart.

5 In a medium bowl, beat the eggs with the sugar, syrup and vanilla. Slowly beat in the melted chocolate.

6 Arrange pecan halves and chocolate chips over bottom of pastry. Place pie plate on baking sheet and carefully pour chocolate-sugar mixture into pastry case. Bake 35–45 minutes, until chocolate mixture is set (top may crack slightly). If pastry edge begins to brown too quickly, cover with strips of foil. Remove to wire rack to cool. Serve warm or chilled, with softly whipped cream.

Double Chocolate Banoffee Pie

The crust can be baked ahead and filled with the toffee and chocolate layers, then refrigerated. Do not add the bananas and cream until a few hours before serving.

Serves 12–14

INGREDIENTS
2 × 400 ml/14 fl oz tins sweetened
  condensed milk
140 g/5 oz bittersweet chocolate,
  broken in pieces
170 ml/5½ fl oz/⅔ cup whipping or
  double cream
10 ml/2 tsp corn or glucose syrup
45 g/1½ oz/3 tbsp unsalted butter, cut
  into pieces
5 ml/1 tsp vanilla essence

GINGER CRUMB CRUST
250 g/9 oz/about 24–26 ginger snaps,
  crushed
85 g/3 oz/6 tbsp butter, melted

TOPPING
140 g/5 oz fine quality white
  chocolate
450 ml/16 fl oz/2 cups double cream
3 ripe bananas
white chocolate curls (optional)
unsweetened cocoa for dusting

bananas

*bittersweet
chocolate*

ginger snaps

white chocolate

1 To make 'toffee', puncture a small hole in each tin. Place the tins in a saucepan large enough to cover with water. Bring water to a boil over medium heat. Reduce heat and simmer 2 hours, partially covered; top up with water if necessary. Remove tins and cool.

   Prepare the crust. Preheat oven to 180°C/350°F/Gas 4. Grease a 23 cm/9 in loose-bottomed tart tin, 4 cm/1½ in deep. Mix ginger snap crumbs with butter and pat on to bottom and side of tin. Bake for 5–7 minutes until set. Cool on rack.

2 In a medium saucepan combine dark chocolate, cream and syrup. Over medium heat, bring to a simmer, stirring frequently until melted and smooth. Remove from heat and beat in butter and vanilla. Pour into cooled crust and refrigerate until set, about 1 hour.

3 Open tins of cooked milk and empty into a bowl. With a wire whisk beat until smooth. Spoon over the chocolate layer. In a food processor with metal disc, process white chocolate into small crumbs. In a saucepan, over medium heat, heat 125 ml/4 fl oz/½ cup of the cream until bubbles form around the edge.

   With machine running, pour in cream and process until chocolate is melted. Strain into a bowl and refrigerate for 25–30 minutes, until cold but not too thick. With an electric mixer, whip remaining cream until stiff. Beat in a spoonful of cream to the chocolate mixture, then fold in remaining cream.

4 Thinly slice the bananas and arrange over toffee layer in crust. Spoon over the chocolate whipped cream, spreading to the edge. Decorate with chocolate curls and a light dusting of cocoa.

Truffle-filled Filo Tulips

The cups can be prepared a day ahead and stored in an airtight container.

Makes about 24 cups

INGREDIENTS
3–6 sheets fresh or frozen (thawed) filo pastry, depending on size
45 g/1½ oz/3 tbsp unsalted butter, melted
sugar for sprinkling
lemon zest to decorate (optional)

CHOCOLATE TRUFFLE MIXTURE
250 ml/8 fl oz/1 cup double cream
225 g/8 oz bittersweet or semi-sweet chocolate, chopped
55 g/2 oz/4 tbsp unsalted butter, cut into pieces
30 ml/2 tbsp brandy or other liqueur

filo pastry

lemon

brandy

bittersweet chocolate

1 Prepare truffle mixture. In a saucepan over medium heat, bring cream to a boil. Remove from heat and add chocolate, stirring until melted. Beat in butter and add brandy. Strain into a bowl. Refrigerate for 1 hour until thick.

2 Preheat oven to 200°C/400°F/Gas 6. Grease a bun tray with 24 × 4 cm/ 1½ in cups. Place filo sheets on a work surface. Cut each sheet into 6 cm/2½ in squares. Cover with damp dish towel. Keeping filo sheets covered, place one square on a work surface. Brush lightly with melted butter, turn over and brush other side. Sprinkle with a pinch of sugar. Butter another square and place it over the first at an angle; sprinkle with sugar. Butter a third square and place over the first two, unevenly, so corners form an uneven edge. Press the layered square into the tray. Continue to fill the tray.

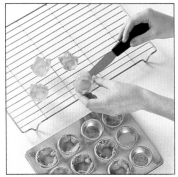

3 Bake the filo cups for 4–6 minutes, until golden. Cool for 10 minutes on a wire rack in the tray. Remove from tray and cool completely.

4 Stir the chocolate mixture; it should be just thick enough to pipe. Spoon mixture into a piping bag with a medium star tip and pipe a swirl into each cup. Decorate each with lemon zest.

Chocolate Lemon Tartlets

Pastry tartlets can be prepared a day ahead but are best filled just a few hours before serving so the fillings are still soft. An easy way to blind bake tartlets is to use paper bun liners. One small liner just covers the bottom and side of a 7.5 cm/3 in tartlet.

Makes 12 tartlets

INGREDIENTS
Follow the pastry recipe on page 36, substituting lemon zest for the orange zest
lemon twists to decorate

LEMON CUSTARD SAUCE
zest and juice of 1 lemon
350 ml/12 fl oz/1½ cups milk
6 egg yolks
55 g/2 oz/⅓ cup caster sugar

LEMON CURD FILLING
grated zest and juice of 2 lemons
170 g/6 oz/¾ cup unsalted butter, cut into pieces
400 g/14 oz/2 cups granulated sugar
3 eggs, lightly beaten

CHOCOLATE LAYER
175 ml/6 fl oz/¾ cup double cream
170 g/6 oz bittersweet or semi-sweet chocolate, chopped
30 g/1 oz/2 tbsp unsalted butter, cut into pieces

lemon

eggs

bittersweet chocolate

1 Prepare custard sauce. Place zest in a saucepan with the milk and over medium heat, bring to the boil. Remove from heat and stand for 5 minutes to infuse. Reheat milk gently. In a bowl with an electric mixer, beat yolks and sugar until pale and thick, 2–3 minutes. Pour over about 250 ml/8 fl oz/1 cup hot milk, beating vigorously. Return yolk mixture to the pan and cook gently, stirring constantly, over low heat, until the mixture thickens and lightly coats back of a spoon. (Do not allow sauce to boil or it will curdle.) Strain into a chilled bowl. Stir 30 ml/2 tbsp lemon juice into sauce. Cool, stirring occasionally, then refrigerate until ready to use.

2 Prepare pastry as on page 36. Prepare lemon curd filling. Combine the lemon zest, juice, butter and sugar in the top of a double boiler. Over medium heat, heat until butter is melted and sugar dissolved. Reduce heat to low. Stir lightly beaten eggs into butter mixture. Cook over low heat, stirring constantly, until mixture thickens and coats the back of a spoon (about 15 minutes). Pour (or strain if you do not want the lemon zest) into a bowl and press clear film against the surface. Cool, stirring occasionally. Refrigerate to thicken, stirring occasionally.

3 Lightly butter 12 × 7.5 cm/3 in tartlet moulds (if possible with removable bases). On a lightly floured surface, roll out pastry to 3 mm/⅛ in thick. Using a 10 cm/4 in fluted-edged cutter, cut out 12 rounds and press each one into tartlet moulds. Prick base. Place moulds on a baking sheet and refrigerate for 30 minutes. Preheat oven to 190°C/375°F/Gas 5. Cut out rounds of foil and line each mould; fill with dry beans or rice. Bake for 5–8 minutes. Remove foil with beans and bake for 5 more minutes, until golden. Remove to rack to cool.

4 Prepare chocolate layer. In a saucepan over medium heat, bring cream to a boil. Remove from heat and add chocolate all at once; stir until melted. Beat in butter and cool slightly. Pour filling into each tartlet to make a layer 5 mm/¼ in thick. Refrigerate for 10 minutes until set. Remove tartlets from moulds and spoon in a layer of lemon curd to come to the top of the pastry. Set aside, but do not refrigerate or chocolate layer will be too firm.

To serve, spoon a little custard on to a plate and place a tartlet in the centre. Decorate with a lemon twist or drop rounds of chocolate in the custard. Draw a skewer through chocolate to make 'heart' motifs.

Rich Chocolate-Berry Tart with Blackberry Sauce

Raspberries, blackberries, alpine strawberries, boysenberries or loganberries, or any combination, can be used to top this tart. Likewise, the sauce can be made with the same berry or from a berry with a complementary flavour.

Serves 10

INGREDIENTS
115 g/4 oz/½ cup unsalted butter, softened
100 g/3½ oz/½ cup caster sugar
2.5 ml/½ tsp salt
15 ml/1 tbsp vanilla essence
55 g/2 oz/½ cup unsweetened cocoa (preferably Dutch-processed)
215 g/7½ oz/1½ cups plain flour
450 g/1 lb fresh berries for topping

CHOCOLATE GANACHE FILLING
450 ml/16 fl oz/2 cups double cream
140 g/5 oz/½ cup seedless blackberry or raspberry preserve
225 g/8 oz bittersweet chocolate, chopped
30 g/1 oz/2 tbsp unsalted butter, cut into pieces

BLACKBERRY SAUCE
225 g/8 oz fresh or frozen blackberries or raspberries
15 ml/1 tbsp lemon juice
30 g/1 oz/2 tbsp caster sugar
30 ml/2 tbsp blackberry or raspberry-flavour liqueur

berries

chocolate

1 Prepare pastry. In a food processor fitted with metal blade, process butter, sugar, salt and vanilla until creamy. Add cocoa and process for 1 minute, until well blended; scrape side of bowl. Add flour all at once and using the pulse action, process for 10–15 seconds, until just blended. Place a piece of clear film on work surface. Remove metal blade and turn out dough on to clear film. Use clear film to help shape dough into flat disc and wrap tightly. Refrigerate for 1 hour.

2 Lightly grease a 23 cm/9 in tart tin with removable base. Soften dough for 5–10 minutes at room temperature. Roll out dough between two sheets of clear film to a 28 cm/11 in round, about 5 mm/¼ in thick. Peel off top sheet of clear film and invert dough into prepared tin. Ease dough into pan. Remove clear film.

3 With floured fingers, press dough on to base and side of tin, then roll rolling pin over edge of tin to cut off any excess dough. Prick base of dough with fork. Refrigerate for 1 hour. Preheat oven to 180°C/350°F/Gas 4. Line tart shell with foil or baking paper; fill with dry beans or rice. Bake for 10 minutes; lift out foil with beans and bake for 5 minutes more, until just set (pastry may look underdone on the bottom, but will dry out). Remove to wire rack to cool completely.

4 Prepare filling. In a medium saucepan over medium heat, bring cream and blackberry preserve to the boil. Remove from heat and add chocolate all at once, stirring until melted and smooth. Stir in butter and strain into cooled tart, smoothing top. Cool tart completely.

5 Prepare sauce. In a food processor combine blackberries, lemon juice and sugar and process until smooth. Strain into a small bowl and add blackberry-flavour liqueur. If sauce is too thick, thin with a little water.

6 To serve, remove tart from tin. Place on serving plate and arrange the berries on the top of the tart. With a pastry brush, brush berries with a little of the blackberry sauce to glaze lightly. Serve remaining sauce separately.

COOK'S TIP
This chocolate pastry has a biscuit-like texture and is difficult to handle. If it is too soft to roll, place the dough into the tin and use lightly floured fingers to press the dough into the bottom and up the side of the tin.

Chocolate Cream Puffs

When making choux pastry, the butter should be completely melted just as the water comes to the boil. Do not allow the water to continue to boil or the proportion of water to flour will not remain accurate.

Makes 12 large or 24 small cream puffs

INGREDIENTS
140 g/5 oz/1 cup plain flour
20 g/1 oz/2 tbsp unsweetened cocoa
250 ml/8 fl oz/1 cup water
2.5 ml/½ tsp salt
15 ml/1 tbsp granulated sugar
115 g/4 oz/½ cup unsalted butter, cut into pieces
4–5 eggs

CHOCOLATE PASTRY CREAM
140 g/5 oz plain chocolate, chopped
450 ml/16 fl oz/2 cups milk
6 egg yolks
100 g/3½ oz/½ cup granulated sugar
50 g/1¾ oz/⅓ cup plain flour
125 ml/4 fl oz/½ cup whipping cream

CHOCOLATE GLAZE
300 ml/10 fl oz/1¼ cups whipping cream
55 g/2 oz/4 tbsp unsalted butter, cut into pieces
225 g/8 oz bittersweet or semi-sweet chocolate, chopped
15 ml/1 tbsp corn or golden syrup
5 ml/1 tsp vanilla essence

1 Preheat oven to 220°C/425°F/Gas 7. Lightly grease 1 or 2 large baking sheets. Into a bowl sift together flour and cocoa. In a saucepan over medium heat, bring to the boil water, salt, sugar and butter (butter should just be melted when water boils). Remove from the heat and add flour mixture all at once, stirring vigorously until flour mixture is well blended and smooth and the mixture pulls away from the side of the pan. Return pan to the heat to cook pastry for 1 minute, beating constantly. Remove from heat.

bittersweet chocolate

eggs

cocoa

2 With an electric mixer (or by hand) beat in four of the eggs, one at a time, beating well after each addition, until each egg is well blended. Mixture should be thick and shiny and just fall from a spoon. If mixture is too dry, beat the fifth egg lightly and add to dough a little at a time until you reach a dropping consistency. Spoon mixture into a large icing bag fitted with a large star or plain tip. Pipe 12 mounds about 7.5 cm/3 in across (or 24 small mounds) at least 5 cm/2 in apart on the baking sheet.

3 Bake for 35–40 minutes until puffed and firm. Remove puffs and turn off oven. Using a serrated knife, slice off top third of puff; return opened puffs, cut-side up, to baking sheet and return to oven for 5–10 minutes to dry out. Remove to wire rack to cool completely.

4 Prepare pastry cream. Melt chocolate and set aside. Over medium heat, bring milk to a boil. In a bowl beat yolks and sugar until pale and thick, 3–5 minutes. Stir in flour. Slowly pour over about 250 ml/8 fl oz/1 cup hot milk into yolks, stirring constantly. Return yolk mixture to the saucepan and cook over medium heat until sauce boils. Cook for 1 minute; remove from heat and quickly stir in melted chocolate until blended.

Strain into a bowl and place a piece of clear film against surface of custard (this prevents a skin forming). Cool to room temperature. Carefully peel clear film from pastry cream. In a bowl with electric mixer, whip cream until firm peaks form. Fold into pastry cream.

5 Spoon pastry cream into a large piping bag fitted with a large star or plain tip. Fill each puff bottom with pastry cream, then cover each puff with its top. Arrange cream puffs on a large serving plate in a single layer or pile them up on top of each other.

6 To serve, in a medium saucepan over low heat, heat the cream, butter, chocolate, syrup and vanilla until melted and smooth, stirring frequently. Remove from heat and cool for 20–30 minutes until slightly thickened. Pour a little sauce over each of the cream puffs and serve while chocolate sauce is warm or refrigerate until ready to serve.

Chocolate Apricot Linzer Tart

To dust the top pastry strips only, cut 1 cm/½ in wide strips of non-stick baking paper at least 28 cm/11 in long and place them between the pastry strips before dusting with icing sugar.

Serves 10–12

INGREDIENTS
70 g/2½ oz/½ cup whole blanched almonds
115 g/4 oz/⅔ cup caster sugar
215 g/7½ oz/1½ cups plain flour
20 g/½ oz/2 tbsp unsweetened cocoa (preferably Dutch-processed)
5 ml/1 tsp ground cinnamon
2.5 ml/½ tsp salt
5 ml/1 tsp grated orange zest
225 g/8 oz/1 cup unsalted butter, cut into pieces
30–45 ml/2–3 tbsp iced water
85 g/3 oz/½ cup plain mini-chocolate chips
icing sugar for dusting

APRICOT FILLING
350 g/12 oz ready-to-eat dried apricots
125 ml/4 fl oz/½ cup orange juice
175 ml/6 fl oz/¾ cup water
45 g/1½ oz/3 tbsp granulated sugar
55 g/2 oz/2 tbsp apricot preserve
2.5 ml/½ tsp ground cinnamon
2.5 ml/½ tsp almond essence

1 Prepare filling. In a large saucepan over medium heat, bring the apricots, orange juice and water to the boil. Lower the heat and simmer gently for 15–20 minutes until the liquid is absorbed, stirring frequently to prevent sticking. Stir in sugar, apricot preserve, cinnamon and almond essence. Press mixture through a strainer into a bowl (or process in a food processor), cool then cover and refrigerate.

2 Prepare pastry. Lightly butter a 28 cm/11 in tart tin with removable base. In a food processor with metal blade, process almonds with half the sugar until finely ground. Into a bowl, sift flour, cocoa, remaining sugar, cinnamon and salt. Add to food processor and process to blend. Add zest and butter and process for

15–20 seconds until mixture resembles coarse crumbs. Add 30 ml/2 tbsp iced water and using pulse action, process until dough just begins to stick together; do not allow dough to form into a ball or pastry will be tough. If dough appears too dry add 15–30 ml/1–2 tbsp more iced water, little by little, until dough holds together.

3 Turn dough on to lightly-floured work surface and knead lightly until just blended. Divide dough in half. With floured fingers, press half the dough on to bottom and side of tin. Prick base of dough with fork. Refrigerate for 30 minutes. Roll out remaining half of dough between 2 sheets of non-stick baking paper or clear film to a 28 cm/11 in round; slide on to a baking sheet and refrigerate for 30 minutes.

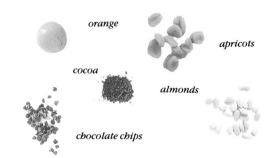

orange

apricots

cocoa

almonds

chocolate chips

 Preheat oven to 180°C/350°F/Gas 4. Spread filling on to base of pastry-lined tin. Sprinkle with chocolate chips. Set aside. Slide dough round on to lightly floured surface and cut into 1 cm/½ in strips; allow to soften for 3–5 minutes.

Place half the dough strips about 1 cm/½ in apart over filling. Place remaining pastry strips diagonally across bottom strips about 1 cm/½ in apart. With fingertips, press down on each side of each crossing to accentuate lattice effect. Press ends to side of tart cutting off any excess.

Bake for 35–40 minutes until top of pastry is set and filling bubbles. Cool on rack to room temperature. To serve, remove side of tin, dust icing sugar over top pastry strips. Slide on to serving plate.

COOK'S TIP

Other dried fruits such as figs, prunes and pears go very well with chocolate. Any of these can be made into a paste as above and used as an alternative filling. For an easy filling, apricot or raspberry jam can be used. If you like, use dark, milk or white chocolate chips for contrast.

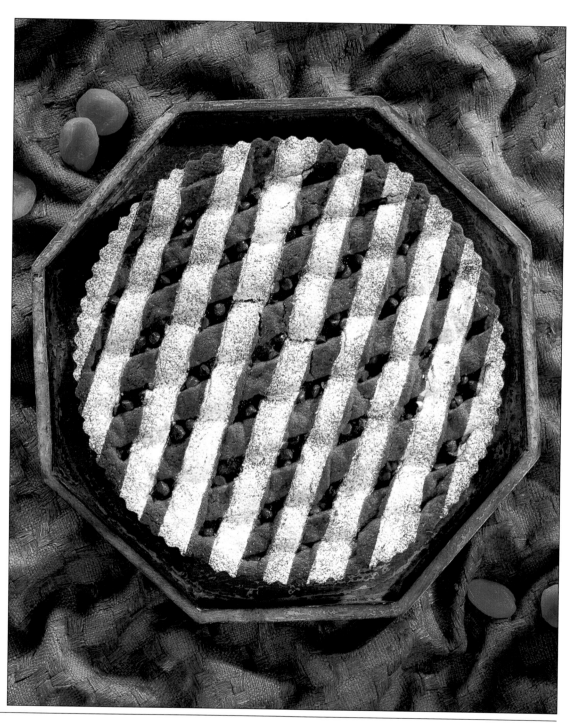

White Chocolate and Mango Cream Tart

To prevent a skin forming on the custard without stirring, dot the top with tiny cubes of butter. When ready to use, simply stir the butter into the custard.

Serves 8

INGREDIENTS
215 g/7½ oz/1½ cups plain flour
130 g/4½ oz/1 cup sweetened, desiccated coconut
115 g/4 oz/½ cup butter, softened
30 ml/2 tbsp caster sugar
2 egg yolks
2.5 ml/½ tsp almond essence
600 ml/1 pint/2½ cups whipping cream
2.5 ml/½ tsp almond essence
55 g/2 oz/⅔ cup flaked almonds, toasted, to decorate

WHITE CHOCOLATE CUSTARD
140 g/5 oz fine quality white chocolate, chopped
125 ml/4 fl oz/½ cup whipping or double cream
35 g/1¼ oz/⅓ cup cornflour
15 ml/1 tbsp plain flour
55 g/2 oz/⅓ cup granulated sugar
350 ml/12 fl oz/1½ cups milk
5 egg yolks
1 large ripe mango

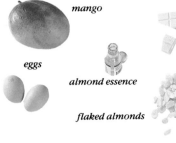

mango

eggs

almond essence

flaked almonds

white chocolate

desiccated coconut

1 In a deep medium mixing bowl, with electric mixer at low speed, combine the flour, coconut, butter, sugar, egg yolks and almond essence until well blended. With fingers or back of a spoon, press pastry on to bottom and side of a lightly buttered 23 cm/9 in tart tin, 4 cm/1½ in deep with removable bottom. Prick base of dough with fork. Refrigerate for 30 minutes.

2 Preheat oven to 180°C/350°F/Gas 4. Line tart shell with foil or non-stick baking paper; fill with dry beans or rice. Bake for 10 minutes. Lift out foil with beans and bake for 5–7 minutes more until golden. Remove to rack to cool completely.

3 Prepare filling. In a small saucepan over low heat, melt white chocolate with the cream, stirring until smooth. Set aside. In a medium saucepan combine the cornflour, flour and sugar. Gradually stir in the milk and cook over medium heat until thickened and bubbling.

4 In a small bowl, beat the egg yolks lightly. Slowly pour over about 250 ml/8 fl oz/1 cup hot milk into the yolks, stirring constantly. Return yolk mixture to the saucepan and bring to a gentle boil, stirring constantly, until thickened. Stir in the melted white chocolate until well blended. Cool to room temperature, stirring frequently to prevent a skin forming on the surface.

5 In a medium bowl with electric mixer, beat the whipping cream and almond essence until soft peaks form. Fold about 125 ml/4 fl oz/½ cup whipped cream into white chocolate custard and spoon half the custard into the base. Peel and slice mango thinly.

6 Arrange the mango slices over the custard and cover with the remaining custard, smoothing top evenly. Remove side of tin and slide on to serving plate. Spoon remaining cream into large piping bag fitted with a medium star tip. Pipe cream in scroll pattern in parallel rows 1 cm/½ in apart. Carefully sprinkle chopped toasted almonds between rows.

Chocolate Tiramisú Tart

This version of the famous Italian dessert, tiramisú (or 'pick-me-up') does not contain coffee-soaked biscuits, as they would cause the crust to become soggy.

Serves 12–16

INGREDIENTS
115 g/4 oz/8 tbsp unsalted butter
15 ml/1 tbsp coffee-flavour liqueur or water
215 g/7½ oz/1½ cups plain flour
30 g/1 oz/¼ cup unsweetened cocoa
30 g/1 oz/¼ cup icing sugar
pinch of salt
2.5 ml/¼ tsp vanilla essence
unsweetened cocoa for dusting

CHOCOLATE LAYER
125 ml/4 fl oz/½ cup double cream
15 ml/1 tbsp light corn or golden syrup
115 g/4 oz bittersweet chocolate, chopped
30 g/1 oz/2 tbsp unsalted butter, cut into pieces
30 ml/1 fl oz/2 tbsp coffee-flavour liqueur

FILLING
250 ml/8 fl oz/1 cup whipping cream
350 g/12 oz mascarpone cheese, at room temperature
20 g/¾ oz/3 tbsp icing sugar
45 ml/1½ fl oz/3 tbsp cold espresso or strong coffee
45 ml/1½ fl oz/3 tbsp coffee-flavour liqueur
100 g/3½ oz semi-sweet chocolate, grated

mascarpone cheese

bittersweet chocolate

1 Prepare pastry. Lightly grease a 23 cm/9 in springform tin. In a saucepan, heat butter and liqueur or water over medium heat until hot. Into a bowl, sift together flour, cocoa, sugar and salt. Remove butter mixture from the heat, stir in vanilla essence and gradually stir into the flour mixture until a soft dough forms. Knead lightly until smooth. Press on to bottom and up side of tin to within 2 cm/¾ in of top. Prick dough. Refrigerate for 40 minutes. Preheat oven to 190°C/375°F/Gas 5. Bake pastry for 8–10 minutes. If pastry puffs up, prick with fork and bake for 2–3 minutes more until set Remove to rack to cool.

2 Prepare chocolate layer. In a saucepan over medium heat, bring cream and syrup to a boil. Remove from heat and add chocolate, stirring until melted. Beat in butter and liqueur and pour into the cooked pastry. Cool completely, then refrigerate.

3 Prepare filling. In a bowl with an electric mixer, whip cream until soft peaks form. In another bowl, beat cheese until soft, then beat in sugar until smooth and creamy. Gradually beat in cold coffee and liqueur; gently fold in whipped cream and chocolate. Spoon filling into the chocolate-lined pastry level with the crust. Refrigerate until ready to serve.

4 To serve, run a sharp knife around the side of the tin to loosen the pastry. Unclip the tin side. Sift a layer of cocoa over the tart.

Chocolate Truffle Tart

Any flavour liqueur can be substituted for brandy – orange, raspberry, coffee and whisky all go very well with chocolate.

Serves 12

INGREDIENTS

150 g/5 oz/1 cup plain flour
30 g/1 oz/⅓ cup unsweetened cocoa (preferably Dutch-processed)
50 g/1¾ oz/¼ cup caster sugar
2.5 ml/½ tsp salt
115 g/4 oz/½ cup cold unsalted butter, cut into pieces
1 egg yolk
15–30 ml/1–2 tbsp iced water
30 g/1 oz fine quality white or milk chocolate, melted
whipped cream for serving (optional)

TRUFFLE FILLING

335 ml/11 fl oz/1⅓ cups double cream
350 g/12 oz couverture or fine quality bittersweet chocolate, chopped
55 g/2 oz/4 tbsp unsalted butter, cut into pieces
30 ml/2 tbsp brandy or other liqueur

bittersweet chocolate

milk chocolate

eggs

brandy

cocoa

1 Prepare pastry. Into a small bowl, sift flour and cocoa. In a food processor fitted with metal blade, process flour mixture, sugar and salt to blend. Add butter and process for 15–20 seconds, until mixture resembles coarse crumbs.

2 In a bowl, lightly beat yolk with iced water. Add to flour mixture and using pulse action, process until dough begins to stick together. Turn out dough on to clear film. Use to help shape dough into flat disc and wrap tightly. Refrigerate for 1–2 hours until firm.

Lightly grease a 23 cm/9 in tart tin with removable base. Soften dough for 5–10 minutes. Roll out dough between sheets of waxed paper or clear film to a 28 cm/22 in round, about 5 mm/¼ in thick. Peel off top sheet and invert dough into pan. Remove bottom sheet. Ease dough on to base and side of tin. Prick base with fork. Refrigerate for 1 hour.

Preheat oven to 180°C/350°F/Gas 4. Line tart with foil or baking paper; fill with dried beans. Bake for 5–7 minutes; lift out foil with beans and bake for 5–7 minutes more, until just set. (Pastry may look slightly underdone on bottom but it will dry out.) Remove to rack to cool.

3 Prepare filling. In a medium saucepan over medium heat, bring cream to the boil. Remove pan from heat and stir in chocolate until melted and smooth. Stir in butter and liqueur. Strain into prepared tart shell, tilting slightly to even surface, but do not touch surface.

4 Spoon melted chocolate into a paper cone and cut tip about 5 mm/¼ in in diameter. Drop rounds of chocolate over surface of tart and with a skewer or toothpick gently draw point through chocolate to produce marbled effect. Refrigerate for 2–3 hours until set. To serve, allow tart to soften slightly at room temperature, about 30 minutes.

Chunky Chocolate Drops

Do not allow these cookies to cool completely on the baking sheet or they will become too crisp and will break when you try to lift them.

Makes about 18 cookies

INGREDIENTS
170 g/6 oz bittersweet or semi-sweet
   chocolate, chopped
125 g/4 oz/½ cup unsalted butter, cut
   into pieces
2 eggs
100 g/3½ oz/½ cup granulated sugar
55 g/2 oz/¼ cup (packed) light
   brown sugar
45 g/1½ oz/⅓ cup plain flour
30 g/1 oz/¼ cup unsweetened cocoa
5 g/1 tsp baking powder
10 ml/2 tsp vanilla essence
pinch of salt
115 g/4 oz/1 cup pecans, toasted and
   coarsely chopped
170 g/6 oz/1 cup semi-sweet
   chocolate chips
115 g/4 oz fine quality white
   chocolate, chopped into 5 mm/¼ in
   pieces
115 g/4 oz fine quality milk chocolate,
   chopped into 5 mm/¼ in pieces

bittersweet chocolate

eggs

cocoa

milk chocolate

white chocolate

pecans

1 Preheat oven to 160°C/325°F/Gas 3. Grease 2 large baking sheets. In a medium saucepan over low heat, melt the bittersweet or semi-sweet chocolate and butter until smooth, stirring frequently. Remove from heat to cool slightly.

2 In a large mixing bowl with electric mixer, beat the eggs and sugars for 2–3 minutes until pale and creamy. Gradually pour in the melted chocolate mixture, beating until well blended. Beat in the flour, cocoa, baking powder, vanilla and salt, until just blended. Stir in the nuts, chocolate chips and chocolate pieces.

3 Drop heaped tablespoons of mixture on to baking sheets 10 cm/4 in apart and flatten each to a round about 7.5 cm/3 in. (You will only get 4–6 cookies on each sheet.) Bake for 8–10 minutes until tops are shiny and cracked and edges look crisp; do not over-bake or cookies will break when removed from baking sheet.

4 Remove baking sheets to wire rack to cool for 2 minutes, until just set, then remove cookies to wire rack to cool completely. Continue to bake in batches. Store in airtight containers.

Chocolate Amaretti

As an alternative decoration, lightly press a few coffee sugar crystals on top of each cookie before baking or dust with icing sugar when cold.

Makes about 24

INGREDIENTS
140 g/5 oz/1 cup blanched whole
   almonds
100 g/3½ oz/½ cup caster sugar
10 g/1 tbsp unsweetened cocoa
20 g/2 tbsp icing sugar
2 egg whites
pinch of cream of tartar
5 ml/1 tsp almond essence
flaked almonds to decorate

eggs

cocoa

almonds

almond essence

1 Preheat oven to 180°C/350°F/Gas 4. Place almonds on a small baking sheet and bake for 10–12 minutes, stirring occasionally, until almonds are golden brown. Remove from oven and cool to room temperature. Reduce oven temperature to 160°C/325°F/Gas 3.

Line a large baking sheet with non-stick baking paper or foil. In a food processor fitted with a metal blade, process the toasted almonds with 50 g/1¾ oz/¼ cup sugar until almonds are finely ground but not oily. Transfer to a medium bowl and sift in the cocoa and icing sugar; stir to blend. Set aside.

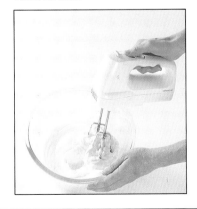

2 In a medium mixing bowl with electric mixer, beat the egg whites and cream of tartar until stiff peaks form. Sprinkle in remaining 50 g/1¾ oz/¼ cup sugar a tablespoon at a time, beating well after each addition, and continue beating until whites are glossy and stiff. Beat in almond essence.

3 Sprinkle over almond-sugar mixture and gently fold into beaten egg whites until just blended. Spoon mixture into a large icing bag fitted with a plain 1 cm/½ in tip. Pipe 4 cm/1½ in rounds about 2.5 cm/1 in apart on prepared baking sheet. Press a flaked almond into the centre of each.

4 Bake cookies for 12–15 minutes or until they appear crisp. Remove baking sheets to wire rack to cool for 10 minutes. With metal palette knife, remove cookies to wire rack to cool completely. When cool, store in an airtight container.

Fudgy Glazed Chocolate Brownies

For a simpler brownie, omit the fudge glaze and dust with icing sugar or cocoa instead.

Serves 8–10

INGREDIENTS

250 g/9 oz bittersweet or semi-sweet chocolate, chopped

30 g/1 oz unsweetened chocolate, chopped

115 g/4 oz/½ cup unsalted butter, cut into pieces

100 g/3½ oz/½ cup (packed) light brown sugar

50 g/1¾ oz/¼ cup granulated sugar

2 eggs

15 ml/1 tbsp vanilla essence

70 g/2½ oz/½ cup plain flour

115 g/4 oz/1 cup pecans or walnuts, toasted and chopped

140 g/5 oz fine quality white chocolate, chopped into 5 mm/¼ in pieces

pecan halves to decorate (optional)

FUDGY CHOCOLATE GLAZE

170 g/6 oz semi-sweet or bittersweet chocolate, chopped

55 g/2 oz/4 tbsp unsalted butter, cut into pieces

30 ml/2 tbsp corn or golden syrup

10 ml/2 tsp vanilla essence

5 ml/1 tsp instant coffee powder

unsweetened chocolate

white chocolate

pecans

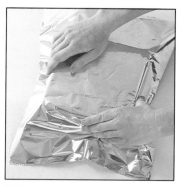

1 Preheat oven to 180°C/350°F/Gas 4. Invert a 20 cm/8 in square baking tin and mould a piece of foil over bottom. Turn tin over and line with moulded foil. Lightly grease foil.

2 In a medium saucepan over a low heat, melt the dark chocolates and butter until smooth, stirring frequently. Remove pan from heat.

3 Stir in sugars and continue stirring for 2 more minutes, until sugar has dissolved. Beat in eggs and vanilla and stir in flour just until blended. Stir in pecans and white chocolate. Pour batter into prepared tin.

4 Bake brownies for 20–25 minutes until a toothpick or cake tester inserted 5 cm/2 in from centre comes out with just a few crumbs attached (do not over-bake). Remove tin to a wire rack to cool for 30 minutes. Using the foil to lift, remove brownies from tin and cool on rack for at least 2 hours.

5 Prepare glaze. In a medium saucepan over medium heat, melt chocolate, butter, syrup, vanilla and coffee powder until smooth, stirring frequently. Remove from heat. Refrigerate for 1 hour or until thickened and spreadable.

6 Invert brownies onto the wire rack, remove foil from bottom. Turn top side up. Using a metal palette knife, spread a thick layer of fudgy glaze over top of brownies just to edges. Refrigerate for 1 hour until set. Cut into squares or 'fingers'. If you wish, top each with a pecan half.

Chocolate Crackle-Tops

These cookies are best eaten as fresh as possible, as they dry slightly on storage, but they will last for several days in an airtight container. Pack them in single layers so the tops are not damaged.

Makes about 38 cookies

INGREDIENTS

200 g/7 oz bittersweet or semi-sweet
   chocolate, chopped
100 g/3½ oz/7 tbsp unsalted butter
115 g/4 oz/⅔ cup caster sugar
3 eggs
5 ml/1 tsp vanilla essence
215 g/7½ oz/1½ cups plain flour
30 g/1 oz/¼ cup unsweetened cocoa
2.5 g/½ tsp baking powder
pinch of salt
170 g/6 oz/1½ cups icing sugar for
   coating

eggs

vanilla essence

bittersweet chocolate

1 Prepare dough. In a medium saucepan over low heat, heat the chocolate and butter until smooth, stirring frequently. Remove from heat. Stir in sugar, continue stirring for 2–3 minutes until sugar dissolves. Add eggs one at a time, beating well after each addition; stir in vanilla. Into a bowl, sift together flour, cocoa, baking powder and salt. Gradually stir into the chocolate mixture in batches, just until blended. Cover dough and refrigerate for at least 1 hour until dough is cold and holds its shape.

2 Preheat oven to 160°C/325°F/Gas 3. Grease 2 or more large baking sheets. Place icing sugar in a small, deep bowl. Using a small ice-cream scoop (about 2.5 cm/1 in diameter) or round teaspoon, scoop cold dough into small balls and, between palms of hands, roll into 4 cm/1½ in balls.

3 Drop balls one at a time into icing sugar and roll until heavily coated. Remove ball with a slotted spoon and tap against side of bowl to remove excess sugar. Place on baking sheets 4 cm/1½ in apart. Use more icing sugar as necessary. (You may need to recycle the baking sheets.)

4 Bake cookies for 10–15 minutes or until top of cookie feels slightly firm when touched with fingertip (do not over-bake or cookies will be dry). Remove baking sheet to wire rack for 2–3 minutes, until just set. With a metal palette knife remove cookies to wire rack to cool completely.

Chocolate Blueberry Muffins

Paper liners not only make for easier washing up, but keep the muffins fresher.

Makes 12

INGREDIENTS
115 g/4 oz/½ cup butter
90 g/3 oz unsweetened chocolate, chopped
200 g/7 oz/1 cup granulated sugar
1 egg, lightly beaten
250 ml/8 fl oz/1 cup buttermilk
10 ml/2 tsp vanilla essence
285 g/10 oz/2 cups plain flour
5 ml/1 tsp bicarbonate of soda
170 g/6 oz/1 cup fresh or frozen blueberries, thawed
30 g/1 oz bittersweet chocolate, melted

bittersweet chocolate

eggs

vanilla essence

unsweetened chocolate

blueberries

1 Preheat oven to 190°C/375°F/Gas 5. In a medium saucepan over medium heat, melt the butter and chocolate until smooth, stirring frequently. Remove from heat to cool slightly.

2 Stir in the sugar, egg, buttermilk and vanilla essence. Gently fold in the flour and bicarbonate of soda until just blended. (Do not overblend; the mixture may be lumpy with some unblended flour.) Fold in the berries.

3 Spoon batter into a greased or paper-lined 6 cm/2½ in bun tray, filling to the top. Bake for 25–30 minutes until a skewer inserted in the centre comes out with just a few crumbs attached. Remove muffins in their paper liners to wire rack immediately (if left in the tin they will go soggy). Drizzle with the melted chocolate and serve warm or cool.

Chocolate Raspberry Macaroon Bars

Any seedless preserve, such as strawberry or apricot, can be substituted for raspberry.

Makes 16–18 bars

INGREDIENTS
115 g/4 oz/½ cup unsalted butter, softened
55 g/2 oz/½ cup icing sugar
30 g/1 oz/⅓ cup unsweetened cocoa (preferably Dutch-processed)
pinch of salt
5 ml/1 tsp almond essence
150 g/5 oz/1 cup plain flour

TOPPING
140 g/5 oz/½ cup seedless raspberry preserve
15 ml/1 tbsp raspberry-flavour liqueur
170 g/6 oz/1 cup mini chocolate chips
170 g/6 oz/1½ cups finely ground almonds
4 egg whites
pinch of salt
200 g/7 oz/1 cup caster sugar
2.5 ml/½ tsp almond essence
55 g/2 oz/⅓ cup flaked almonds

raspberry preserve

eggs

chocolate chips

1 Preheat oven to 160°C/325°F/Gas 3. Invert a 23 × 33 cm/9 × 13 in baking tin. Mould a sheet of foil over tin and smooth foil evenly around corners. Lift off foil and turn tin right side up; line with moulded foil. Grease foil.

2 In a medium bowl with an electric mixer, beat together the butter, sugar, cocoa and salt until well blended, about 1 minute. Beat in the almond essence and the flour until mixture forms a crumbly dough.

3 Turn dough into the prepared tin and pat firmly over bottom to make an even layer. Prick dough with a fork. Bake for 20 minutes until just set. Remove from oven and increase temperature to 190°C/375°F/Gas 5.

4 In a small bowl, combine the raspberry preserve and raspberry-flavour liqueur. Spread evenly over chocolate crust, then sprinkle evenly with the chocolate chips.

5 In a food processor fitted with a metal blade, process the almonds, egg whites, salt, sugar and almond essence until well blended and foamy. Gently pour over jam layer, spreading evenly to edges of tin. Sprinkle with flaked almonds.

6 Bake for 20–25 minutes more until top is golden and puffed. Remove to wire rack to cool in tin for 20 minutes or until firm. Using edges of foil, carefully remove from tin and cool completely. Peel off foil and, using a sharp knife, cut into bars.

Black and White Ginger Florentines

These florentines can be refrigerated in an airtight container for one week.

Makes about 30

INGREDIENTS

125 ml/4 fl oz/½ cup double cream
55 g/2 oz/¼ cup unsalted butter
100 g/3½ oz/½ cup granulated sugar
30 ml/2 tbsp honey
140 g/5 oz/1⅔ cups flaked almonds
45 g/1½ oz/⅓ cup plain flour
25 ml/½ tsp ground ginger
55 g/2 oz/⅓ cup diced candied orange peel
70 g/2½ oz/½ cup diced stem ginger
55 g/2 oz semi-sweet chocolate, chopped
140 g/5 oz bittersweet chocolate, chopped
140 g/5 oz fine quality white chocolate, chopped

bittersweet chocolate

honey

candied orange peel

white chocolate

flaked almonds

1 Preheat oven to 180°C/350°F/Gas 4. Lightly grease 2 large baking sheets. (Non-stick sheets are ideal for these caramel-like cookies.) In a medium saucepan over medium heat, stir cream, butter, sugar and honey until sugar dissolves. Bring mixture to the boil, stirring constantly. Remove from heat and stir in almonds, flour and ground ginger until well blended. Stir in orange peel, stem ginger and chopped semi-sweet chocolate.

2 Drop teaspoons of mixture on to prepared sheets at least 7.5 cm/3 in apart. Spread each round as thinly as possible with the back of the spoon. (Dip spoon into water to prevent sticking.)

3 Bake for 8–10 minutes or until edges are golden brown and biscuits are bubbling. Do not underbake or they will be sticky, but be careful not to over-bake as the high sugar and fat content allows them to burn easily. Continue baking in batches. If you wish, use a 7.5 cm/3 in biscuit cutter to neaten the edges of the florentines while on the baking sheet.

4 Remove to wire rack to cool for 10 minutes until firm. Using a metal palette knife, carefully remove cookies to wire rack to cool completely.

5 In a small saucepan over very low heat, heat the bittersweet chocolate, stirring frequently, until melted and smooth. Cool slightly. In the top of a double boiler over low heat, melt the white chocolate until smooth, stirring frequently. Remove top of double boiler from bottom and cool for about 5 minutes, stirring occasionally until slightly thickened.

6 Using a small metal palette knife, spread half the florentines with the bittersweet chocolate on flat side of each biscuit, swirling to create a decorative surface, and place on wire rack, chocolate side up. Spread remaining florentines with the melted white chocolate and place on rack, chocolate side up. Refrigerate for 10–15 minutes to set completely.

White Chocolate Brownies with Milk Chocolate Macadamia Topping

If you wish, hazelnuts can be substituted for the macadamia nuts in the topping.

Serves 12

INGREDIENTS
150 g/5 oz/1 cup plain flour
2.5 ml/½ tsp baking powder
pinch of salt
170 g/6 oz fine quality white
   chocolate, chopped
100 g/3½ oz/½ cup caster sugar
115 g/4 oz/½ cup unsalted butter, cut
   into pieces
2 eggs, lightly beaten
5 ml/1 tsp vanilla essence
170 g/6 oz semi-sweet chocolate
   chips or semi-sweet chocolate,
   chopped

TOPPING
200 g/7 oz milk chocolate, chopped
210 g/7½ oz/1 cup unsalted
   macadamia nuts, chopped

milk chocolate

macadamia nuts

1 Preheat oven to 180°C/350°F/Gas 4. Grease a 23 cm/9 in springform tin. Sift together the flour, baking powder and salt, set aside.

2 In a medium saucepan over medium heat, melt the white chocolate, sugar and butter until smooth, stirring frequently. Cool slightly, then beat in the eggs and vanilla. Stir in the flour until well blended. Stir in the chocolate chips or chopped chocolate. Spread evenly in the prepared tin, smoothing top.

3 Bake for 20–25 minutes until a toothpick inserted 5 cm/2 in from side of tin comes out clean; do not over-bake. Remove from the oven to a heatproof surface. Immediately sprinkle chopped milk chocolate evenly over surface (avoid touching the side of tin) and return to oven for 1 minute.

4 Remove from oven and, using the back of a spoon, gently spread the softened chocolate evenly over the top. Sprinkle with the macadamia nuts and gently press into chocolate. Cool on wire rack 30 minutes, then refrigerate until set, about 1 hour. Run a sharp knife around the side of the tin to loosen; then unclip springform tin side and carefully remove. Cut into thin wedges.

Chocolate-dipped Hazelnut Crescents

Walnuts or pecans can be used instead of hazelnuts, but they must be finely ground.

Makes about 35

INGREDIENTS

285 g/10 oz/2 cups plain flour
pinch of salt
225 g/8 oz/1 cup unsalted butter,
  softened
55 g/2 oz/⅓ cup caster sugar
15 ml/1 tbsp hazelnut liqueur or
  water
5 ml/1 tsp vanilla essence
85 g/3 oz/½ cup semi-sweet
  chocolate, finely grated
70 g/2½ oz/½ cup hazelnuts, toasted
  and finely chopped
icing sugar for dusting
350 g/12 oz semi-sweet chocolate,
  melted, for dipping

semi-sweet chocolate

hazelnuts

vanilla essence

1 Preheat oven to 160°C/325°F/Gas 3. Grease 2 large baking sheets. Sift the flour and salt into a bowl.

2 In a large bowl with an electric mixer, beat the butter until creamy, about 1 minute. Add the sugar and beat until fluffy, beat in the hazelnut liqueur and vanilla. Gently stir in the flour, until just blended, then fold in the grated chocolate and hazelnuts.

3 With floured hands, shape the dough into 5 × 1 cm/2 × ½ in crescent shapes. Place on baking sheets, 5 cm/2 in apart. Bake for 20–25 minutes until edges are set and the biscuits slightly golden. Remove baking sheets to rack to cool for 10 minutes. Transfer biscuits from baking sheets to racks to cool completely.

4 Dust biscuits with icing sugar. Using a pair of kitchen tongs or fingers dip half of each crescent into melted chocolate. Place on non-stick baking paper-lined baking sheet and cool. Chill until the chocolate has set.

Chocolate Soufflé Crêpes

A non-stick pan is ideal as it does not need greasing between each crêpe. Serve two crêpes per person.

Makes 12 crêpes

INGREDIENTS
75 g/2¾ oz/7 tbsp plain flour
10 g/¼ oz/1 tbsp unsweetened cocoa
5 ml/1 tsp caster sugar
pinch of salt
5 ml/1 tsp ground cinnamon
2 eggs
175 ml/6 fl oz/¾ cup milk
5 ml/1 tsp vanilla essence
55 g/2 oz/4 tbsp unsalted butter, melted
icing sugar for dusting
raspberries, pineapple and mint sprigs to decorate

PINEAPPLE SYRUP
½ medium pineapple, peeled, cored and finely chopped
125 ml/4 fl oz/½ cup water
30 ml/2 tbsp natural maple syrup
5 ml/1 tsp cornflour
½ cinnamon stick
30 ml/2 tbsp rum

SOUFFLÉ FILLING
250 g/9 oz semi-sweet or bittersweet chocolate
85 ml/3 fl oz/⅓ cup double cream
3 eggs, separated
30 g/1 oz/2 tbsp caster sugar

bittersweet chocolate

mint sprigs

cinnamon stick

raspberries

1 Prepare syrup. In a saucepan over medium heat, bring pineapple, water, maple syrup, cornflour and cinnamon stick to the boil. Simmer for 2–3 minutes until sauce thickens, whisking frequently. Remove from heat; discard cinnamon. Pour into a bowl, stir in rum and chill.

4 Prepare filling. In a small saucepan, over medium heat, melt chocolate and cream until smooth, stirring frequently.

2 Prepare crêpes. In a bowl, sift flour, cocoa, sugar, salt and cinnamon. Stir to blend, then make a well in the centre. In a bowl, beat eggs, milk and vanilla and gradually add to the well in the flour mixture, whisking in flour from the side of the bowl to form a smooth batter. Stir in half the melted butter and pour batter into a jug. Allow to stand 1 hour.

5 In a bowl, with electric mixer, beat yolks with half the sugar for 3–5 minutes, until light and creamy. Gradually beat in the chocolate mixture. Allow to cool. In a large bowl with cleaned beaters, beat egg whites until soft peaks form. Gradually beat in remaining sugar until stiff peaks form. Beat in a large spoonful of whites to the chocolate mixture to lighten it, then fold in remaining whites.

3 Heat an 18–20 cm/7–8 in crêpe pan. Brush with butter. Stir the batter. Pour 45 ml/3 tbsp batter into the pan; swirl pan quickly to cover bottom with a thin layer. Cook over medium-high heat for 1–2 minutes until bottom is golden. Turn over and cook for 30–45 seconds, then turn on to a plate. Stack crêpes between non-stick baking paper and set aside.

6 Preheat oven to 200°C/400°F/Gas 6. Lay a crêpe on a plate, bottom side up. Spoon a little soufflé mixture on to crêpe, spreading it to the edge. Fold the bottom half over the soufflé mixture, then fold in half again to form a filled 'triangle'. Place on a buttered baking sheet. Repeat with remaining crêpes. Brush the tops with melted butter and bake for 15–20 minutes until filling has souffléd. Garnish with mint and a spoonful of syrup.

Luxury Mocha Mousse

As a variation, use an orange-flavour liqueur, brandy or even water in place of the coffee.

Serves 6

INGREDIENTS
225 g/8 oz fine quality bittersweet
  chocolate, chopped
65 ml/2 fl oz/¼ cup espresso or
  strong coffee
30 g/1 oz/2 tbsp butter, cut into
  pieces
30 ml/2 tbsp brandy or rum
3 eggs, separated
pinch of salt
45 g/1½ oz/3 tbsp caster sugar
125 ml/4 fl oz/½ cup whipping cream
30 ml/2 tbsp coffee-flavour liqueur
chocolate coffee beans to decorate
  (optional)

bittersweet
chocolate

eggs

chocolate coffee beans

1 In a medium saucepan over medium heat, melt the chocolate and coffee, stirring frequently until smooth. Remove from the heat and beat in the butter and brandy or rum.

2 In a small bowl, beat the yolks lightly then beat into the melted chocolate; the mixture will thicken. Cool. In a large bowl with electric mixer, beat the whites to 'break' them. Add a pinch of salt and beat on medium speed until soft peaks form. Increase speed and beat until stiff peaks form. Beat in sugar, 1 tbsp at a time, beating well after each addition until whites are glossy and stiff, but not dry.

3 Beat 1 large spoonful of whites into chocolate mixture to lighten it, then fold chocolate into remaining whites. Pour into a large glass serving bowl or 6 individual dishes and refrigerate for at least 3–4 hours before serving.

4 In a medium bowl, beat the cream and coffee-flavour liqueur until soft peaks form. Spoon into an icing bag fitted with a medium star tip and pipe rosettes or shells on to surface of mousse. Garnish with a chocolate coffee bean.

Chocolate Pavlova with Chocolate Curls and Fruits

Do not attempt to make meringues on a hot humid day, as the moisture can make the meringue go sticky or 'weep'.

Serves 8–10

INGREDIENTS
255 g/10 oz/2¼ cups icing sugar
10 g/¼ oz/1 tbsp unsweetened cocoa
5 g/1 tsp cornflour
5 egg whites at room temperature
pinch of salt
5 ml/1 tsp cider vinegar or lemon juice

CHOCOLATE CREAM
170 g/6 oz bittersweet or semi-sweet chocolate, chopped
125 ml/4 fl oz/½ cup milk
30 g/1 oz/2 tbsp unsalted butter, cut into pieces
30 ml/2 tbsp brandy
450 ml/16 fl oz/2 cups double or whipping cream

TOPPING
chocolate curls to decorate
450 g/1 lb/2 cups mixed berries or cut-up fruits such as mango, papaya, fresh lychees and pineapple
icing sugar to decorate

bittersweet chocolate

eggs

mixed berries

1 Prepare meringue. Preheat oven to 160°C/325°F/Gas 3. Place a sheet of non-stick baking paper on a baking sheet and mark a 20 cm/8 in circle on it. In a small bowl, sift together 3 tbsp of icing sugar, with the cocoa and cornflour. In a mixing bowl with electric mixer, beat egg whites until frothy. Add salt and beat until whites form stiff peaks. Sprinkle in the remaining icing sugar, a little at a time, making sure each addition is dissolved before adding the next. Fold in sugar mixture; then quickly fold in vinegar or lemon juice.

2 Spoon the mixture on to the circle on the paper, building up the sides higher than the centre. Bake in the centre of the oven for 1 hour until set. Turn off oven and allow the meringue to stand in the oven for 1 hour longer (the meringue may crack or sink). Remove from oven and cool.

3 Prepare the chocolate cream. In a medium saucepan over low heat, melt the chocolate and milk, stirring until smooth. Remove from the heat and whisk in the butter and brandy and cool for 1 hour.

4 Using a metal palette knife, transfer meringue to a serving plate. Cut a circle around the centre of the meringue about 5 cm/2 in from the edge to allow the centre to sink without pulling edges in. When chocolate mixture has cooled, but is not too firm, in a medium bowl with electric mixer beat the cream until soft peaks form. Stir half the cream into the chocolate to lighten it, then fold in remaining cream. Spoon into the centre of the meringue. Arrange chocolate curls and fruit in the centre of the meringue, over the cream. Dust with icing sugar.

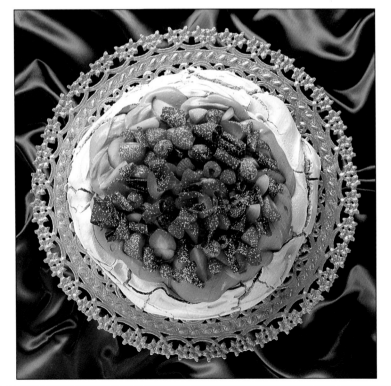

Hazelnut Chocolate Meringue Torte with Pears

Do not assemble this torte more than 3–4 hours before serving, as the pears may give off liquid and soften the cream too much.

Serves 8–10

INGREDIENTS
140 g/5 oz/¾ cup granulated sugar
1 vanilla bean, split
450 ml/16 fl oz/2 cups water
4 ripe pears, peeled, halved and cored
30 ml/1 fl oz/2 tbsp pear or hazelnut-flavour liqueur
180 g/6½ oz/1¼ cups hazelnuts, toasted
6 egg whites
pinch of salt
350 g/12 oz/2½ cups icing sugar
5 ml/1 tsp vanilla essence
55 g/2 oz semi-sweet chocolate, melted

CHOCOLATE CREAM
285 g/10 oz fine quality bittersweet or semi-sweet chocolate, chopped
450 ml/16 fl oz/2 cups whipping cream
65 ml/2 fl oz/¼ cup pear or hazelnut-flavour liqueur

bittersweet chocolate

eggs

hazelnut-flavour liqueur

pears

hazelnuts

1 In a saucepan large enough to hold the pears in a single layer combine sugar, vanilla bean and water. Over high heat, bring to the boil, stirring until sugar dissolves. Reduce heat to medium. Lower pears into the syrup. Cover pears and simmer gently for 12–15 minutes until tender. Remove pan from heat and allow pears to cool in their poaching liquid. Carefully remove pears from liquid. Drain. Place on a flat plate lined with layers of kitchen paper. Sprinkle each half with the liqueur. Cover and refrigerate overnight.

4 Prepare chocolate cream. Place chocolate in a small bowl. Set bowl over a pan of simmering water, turn off heat. Stir chocolate until melted and smooth. Cool chocolate to room temperature. In a bowl with electric mixer, beat cream to soft peaks. Quickly fold cream into melted chocolate; fold in liqueur. Spoon about one third of chocolate cream into an icing bag fitted with a star tip. Set aside.

2 Preheat oven to 180°C/350°F/Gas 4. With a pencil draw a 23 cm/9 in circle in the centre of each of 2 sheets of non-stick baking paper or well greased foil. Turn paper over on to 2 baking sheets (so pencil marks are underneath) or slide foil on to baking sheets. In a food processor fitted with metal blade, process the toasted hazelnuts until medium-fine crumbs form.

3 In a large bowl with an electric mixer on medium, beat the whites until frothy. Add salt and beat on high speed until soft peaks form. Reduce mixer speed and gradually add sugar, beating well after each addition until all the sugar is added and whites are stiff and glossy; this takes 12–15 minutes. Gently fold in nuts and vanilla and spoon meringue on to baking sheets, spreading into 23 cm/9 in circles, smoothing top and sides. Bake for 1 hour until tops are dry and firm. Turn off oven and allow to cool in the oven, 2–3 hours or overnight, until completely dry.

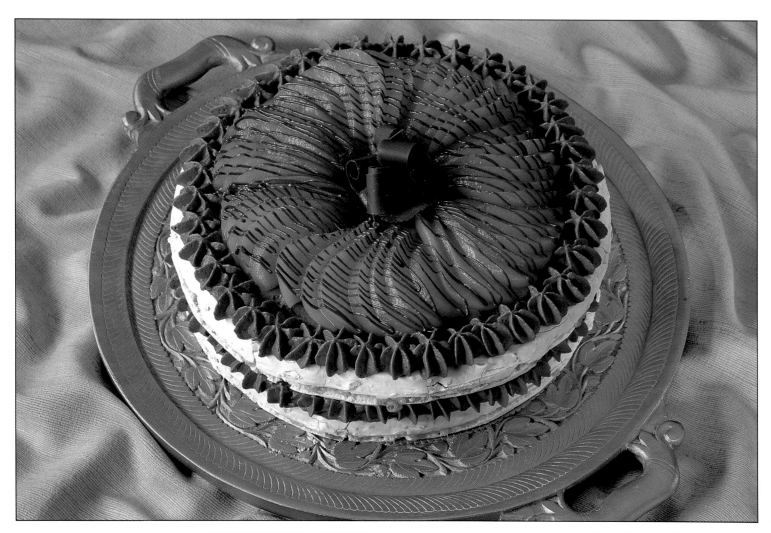

5 To assemble, with a sharp knife, thinly slice each pear half lengthwise. Place one meringue layer on a serving plate. Spread with half the chocolate cream and arrange half the sliced pears evenly over the cream. Pipe a border of rosettes around the edge.

6 Top with the second meringue layer and spread with the remaining chocolate cream. Arrange the remaining pear slices in an attractive pattern over the chocolate cream. Pipe a border of rosettes around the edge. Spoon the melted chocolate into a small paper cone and drizzle the chocolate over the pears. Refrigerate for at least 1 hour before serving.

White Chocolate Hearts with Two Sauces

The caramel nests should not be made more than a few hours before serving, as the sugar begins to soften fairly quickly.

Serves 6

INGREDIENTS
350 ml/11 fl oz/1⅓ cups whipping
cream
115 g/4 oz fine quality white
chocolate, chopped
10 ml/2 tsp/⅔ packet unflavoured
gelatin
65 ml/2 fl oz/¼ cup water
250 ml/8 fl oz/1 cup milk
4 egg yolks
50 g/1¾ oz/¼ cup granulated sugar
30 ml/1 fl oz/2 tbsp orange-flavour
liqueur
4 small satsumas or tangerines, peeled
and sectioned
6 kumquats, thinly sliced

CARAMEL SAUCE
250 g/9 oz/1⅓ cup granulated or
lump sugar
275 ml/9 fl oz/1⅓ cup water

CHOCOLATE SAUCE
225 g/8 oz fine quality bittersweet
chocolate, chopped
55 g/2 oz/¼ cup unsalted butter, cut
into pieces
175 ml/6 fl oz/¾ cup water
30 ml/2 tbsp brandy or chocolate-
flavour liqueur

CARAMEL NESTS (OPTIONAL)
115 g/4 oz granulated or lump sugar
65 ml/2 fl oz/¼ cup water
30 ml/2 tbsp liquid glucose (available
from chemists) or corn syrup

1 Lightly oil 6 × 125 ml/4 fl oz/½ cup heart-shaped or other moulds. In a small saucepan over low heat, bring 85 ml/ 3 fl oz/⅓ cup cream to a boil. Add the white chocolate all at once, stirring constantly until smooth. Set aside. Sprinkle gelatin over water in a small bowl; allow to stand and soften.

bittersweet chocolate

kumquats

satsumas

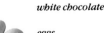
white chocolate

eggs

2 In a medium saucepan over medium heat, bring milk to a boil. In a medium bowl with a hand-held electric mixer, beat the egg yolks and sugar until thick and pale, 2–3 minutes. Reduce mixer to lowest speed; gradually beat in milk, then return custard mixture to saucepan.

3 Cook custard over medium heat, stirring constantly with a wooden spoon until mixture thickens slightly and coats the back of the spoon. (Do not boil or custard will curdle.) Remove from the heat and stir in softened gelatin until completely dissolved; then stir into the chocolate mixture. Strain custard into a large chilled jug. Stir in orange-flavour liqueur and refrigerate for about 20 minutes until mixture begins to thicken, stirring occasionally.

4 In a mixing bowl with electric mixer, beat remaining 250 ml/8 fl oz/1 cup cream until soft peaks form. Gently fold into the thickening custard mixture. Carefully pour into moulds. Place moulds on baking sheet and refrigerate for 2 hours or until set. Cover moulds with clear film and refrigerate for several hours or overnight. (Unmould desserts at least 30 minutes before serving to soften slightly.)
Prepare caramel sauce. Place sugar and

half the water into a heavy-bottomed saucepan. Stir over medium heat until sugar dissolves. Increase heat and boil, swirling pan occasionally until syrup turns light brown, 3–4 minutes. Remove from heat and, standing back from pan, carefully pour in remaining water (mixture will spit). Return to heat and simmer gently until caramel dissolves, stirring occasionally. Cool then pour into serving boat and keep at room temperature.

5 Prepare chocolate sauce. In medium saucepan over medium heat, melt the chocolate, butter and water until smooth, stirring frequently. Remove from heat and cool slightly. Stir in brandy or liqueur and strain into sauceboat; cool to room temperature. (Sauce can be made ahead, but may solidify if refrigerated. Heat gently then cool before serving.)

6 To serve, fill a tart tin or soup bowl with hot water. Run a sharp knife around the edge of each mould and dip into the hot water for 4–6 seconds. Dry bottom of mould; quickly cover dessert with a plate. Invert mould on to plate, giving a firm shake; carefully remove mould. Spoon a little of each sauce around each heart-shaped cream and arrange fruits on plates. If you like, garnish with caramel nests and serve with additional sauce.

CARAMEL NESTS

Wrap a rolling pin in foil and brush lightly with oil. Place on a lightly oiled baking sheet. Tape together 2 long tined forks.

In a small heavy-based saucepan over medium heat, swirl the sugar and water until dissolved. Bring to the boil and add the glucose or syrup, swirl to blend. Half cover the pan and boil until the syrup turns a light caramel brown, about 3–4 minutes. Immediately dip the base of the pan into ice cold water to stop cooking.

Dip the forks into the caramel and holding the rolling pin over the baking sheet, sharply flick the fork backwards and forwards over the pin to form long, thin strands of sugar. Repeat by dipping forks with syrup and flicking. Cut spun sugar into pieces and mould over dessert plates.

Chocolate Amaretto Marquise

A 23 cm/9 in springform cake tin is ideal for this recipe, but for special occasions it is worth taking extra time to line a heart-shaped tin carefully.

Serves 10–12

INGREDIENTS

15 ml/1 tbsp flavourless vegetable oil, such as groundnut or sunflower
85 g/3 oz/7–8 amaretti biscuits, finely crushed
30 g/1 oz/2 tbsp unblanched almonds, toasted and finely chopped
450 g/1 lb fine quality bittersweet or semi-sweet chocolate, broken into pieces or chopped
75 ml/2½ fl oz/⅓ cup Amaretto liqueur
75 ml/2½ fl oz/⅓ cup corn syrup or golden syrup
500 ml/16 fl oz/2 cups double cream
unsweetened cocoa for dusting

AMARETTO CREAM (OPTIONAL)

350 ml/12 fl oz/1½ cups whipping or double cream for serving
30–45 ml/2–3 tbsp Amaretto liqueur

bittersweet chocolate

amaretti biscuits

Amaretto liqueur

almonds

1 Lightly oil a 23 cm/9 in heart-shaped or springform cake tin. Line the bottom with non-stick baking paper and oil the paper. In a small bowl, combine the crushed amaretti biscuits and the chopped almonds. Sprinkle evenly on to the bottom of the tin.

2 Place the chocolate, Amaretto liqueur and corn syrup in a medium saucepan over a very low heat. Stir frequently until chocolate is melted and mixture is smooth. Allow to cool until mixture feels just warm to the touch, about 6–8 minutes.

3 In a bowl with electric mixer, beat the cream until it just begins to hold its shape. Stir a large spoonful into the chocolate mixture, then quickly add remaining cream and gently fold into the chocolate mixture. Pour into the prepared tin and tap tin gently on the work surface to release any large air bubbles. Cover the tin with clear film and refrigerate overnight.

4 To unmould, run a thin-bladed sharp knife under hot water and dry carefully. Run the knife around the edge of the tin to loosen dessert. Place a serving plate over the tin, then invert to unmould the dessert. Carefully peel off the paper, replacing any crust that sticks to it, and dust with cocoa. To serve, whip the cream and Amaretto liqueur until soft peaks form and serve separately.

Double Chocolate Snowball

This is an ideal party dessert as it can be prepared at least one day ahead and decorated on the day.

Serves 12–14

INGREDIENTS

350 g/12 oz bittersweet or semi-sweet
   chocolate, chopped
300 g/10½ oz/1½ cups caster sugar
285 g/10 oz/1¼ cups unsalted butter,
   cut into small pieces
8 eggs
60 ml/2 fl oz/¼ cup orange-flavoured
   liqueur or brandy (optional)
cocoa for dusting

WHITE CHOCOLATE CREAM
200 g/7 oz fine quality white
   chocolate, broken into pieces
450 ml/16 fl oz/2 cups double or
   whipping cream
30 ml/1 fl oz/1 tbsp orange-flavour
   liqueur (optional)

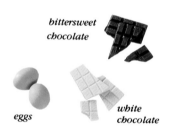

*bittersweet
chocolate*

eggs

*white
chocolate*

1 Preheat the oven to 180°C/350°F/
Gas 4. Line a 1.75 litre/3 pint/1½ quart
round ovenproof bowl with aluminium
foil, smoothing the sides. In a bowl over a
pan of simmering water, melt the
bittersweet or semi-sweet chocolate.
Add sugar and stir until chocolate is
melted and sugar dissolves. Strain into a
medium bowl. With an electric mixer at
low speed, beat in the butter, then the
eggs, one at a time, beating well after each
addition. Stir in the liqueur or brandy and
pour into the prepared bowl. Tap gently
to release any large air bubbles.

2 Bake for 1¼–1½ hours until the
surface is firm and slightly risen, but
cracked. The centre will still be wobbly:
this will set on cooling. Remove to rack to
cool to room temperature; the top will
sink. Cover with a dinner plate (to make
an even surface for unmoulding); then
cover completely with clear film or foil
and refrigerate overnight. To unmould,
remove plate and film or foil and place a
serving plate over the top of the mould.
Invert mould on to plate and shake firmly
to release the dessert. Carefully peel off
foil. Cover until ready to decorate.

3 In a food processor fitted with a
metal blade, process the white chocolate
until fine crumbs form. In a small
saucepan, heat 125 ml/4 fl oz/½ cup
cream until just beginning to simmer.
With the food processor running, pour
cream through the feed tube and process
until the chocolate is completely melted.
Strain into a medium bowl and cool to
room temperature, stirring occasionally.

4 In another bowl, with the electric
mixer, beat the cream until soft peaks
form, add liqueur and beat for 30 seconds
or until cream holds its shape, but not
until stiff. Fold a spoonful of cream into
the chocolate mixture to lighten it, then
fold in remaining cream. Spoon into an
icing bag fitted with a star tip and pipe
rosettes over the surface. If you wish, dust
with cocoa.

White Chocolate Raspberry Ripple Ice Cream

Freeze ice cream in a soufflé dish or other attractive bowl so it can be served directly at the table.

Makes 1 litre/1¾ pints

INGREDIENTS
250 ml/8 fl oz/1 cup milk
450 ml/16 fl oz/2 cups whipping
   cream
7 egg yolks
30 g/1 oz/2 tbsp granulated sugar
225 g/8 oz fine quality white
   chocolate, chopped
5 ml/1 tsp vanilla essence
mint sprigs to decorate

RASPBERRY RIPPLE SAUCE
285 g/10 oz packet frozen raspberries
   in light syrup or 285 g/10 oz jar
   reduced sugar raspberry preserve
10 ml/2 tsp corn syrup
15 ml/1 tbsp lemon juice
10 ml/1 tbsp cornflour diluted in
   15 ml/1 tbsp water

raspberries

eggs

white chocolate

lemon

1 Prepare sauce. Press raspberries and their syrup through a sieve into a saucepan. Add corn syrup, lemon juice and dissolved cornflour. (If using preserve, omit cornflour, but add the water.) Bring to the boil, stirring frequently, and simmer for 1–2 minutes until syrupy. Pour into a bowl and cool, then refrigerate.

2 In a pan, combine milk and 250 ml/ 8 fl oz/1 cup cream and bring to the boil. In a bowl with a hand-held mixer, beat yolks and sugar until thick and creamy, 2–3 minutes. Gradually pour hot milk over yolks and return to pan. Cook over medium heat until custard coats back of a wooden spoon, stirring constantly. (Do not boil or custard will curdle.)

3 Remove pan from heat and stir in the white chocolate until melted and smooth. Pour remaining cream into a large bowl. Strain the hot custard into bowl with cream and vanilla. Blend well and cool to room temperature. Refrigerate until cold. Transfer custard to an ice cream maker and freeze according to manufacturer's instructions.

4 When mixture is frozen, but still soft, transfer one third of the ice cream to a bowl. Spoon over some raspberry sauce. Cover with another third of the ice cream and more sauce. Cover with remaining ice cream and more sauce. With a knife or spoon, lightly marble sauce into the ice cream. Cover and freeze. Allow ice cream to soften for 20–30 minutes in the refrigerator before serving with remaining raspberry sauce.

French-style Coupe Glacée with Chocolate Ice Cream

This dessert can be made with a good quality bought ice cream, but this extra rich chocolate ice cream is the main feature.

Serves 6–8

INGREDIENTS
225 g/8 oz bittersweet chocolate, chopped
250 ml/8 fl oz/1 cup milk mixed with 250 ml/8 fl oz/1 cup single cream
3 egg yolks
50 g/1¾ oz/¼ cup granulated sugar
350 ml/12 fl oz/1½ cups double cream
15 ml/1 tbsp vanilla essence
chocolate triangles to decorate

ESPRESSO CREAM
45 g/3 tbsp instant espresso powder, dissolved in 45 ml/3 tbsp boiling water, cooled
350 ml/12 fl oz/1½ cups double cream
30 ml/2 tbsp coffee-flavour liqueur

CHOCOLATE ESPRESSO SAUCE
300 ml/10 fl oz/1¼ cups double cream
30 g/2 tbsp instant espresso powder, dissolved in 45 ml/3 tbsp boiling water
320 g/11 oz bittersweet chocolate, chopped
30 ml/2 tbsp coffee-flavour liqueur

bittersweet chocolate

espresso powder

1 Prepare ice cream. In a saucepan over a low heat, melt the chocolate with 125 ml/4 fl oz/½ cup of milk mixture, stirring frequently. Remove from heat. In a saucepan over medium heat, bring to a boil remaining milk mixture. In a mixing bowl with a hand-held mixer, beat yolks and sugar until thick and creamy, 2–3 minutes. Gradually pour hot milk mixture over yolks, whisking constantly, and return mixture to pan. Cook over medium heat until custard thickens, stirring constantly. (Do not boil or custard will curdle.) Immediately pour over melted chocolate, stirring until blended.

2 Pour cream into a bowl and strain custard into bowl with vanilla. Blend and cool to room temperature. Refrigerate until cold. Transfer to an ice cream maker and freeze according to instructions.

3 Meanwhile, prepare espresso cream. In a large bowl stir the cooled, dissolved espresso powder into the cream. With an electric mixer, beat the cream until it holds soft peaks. Beat in the liqueur and beat for 30 seconds longer. Spoon cream into an icing bag fitted with a medium star tip and refrigerate until ready to assemble dessert.

4 Prepare sauce. In a saucepan over medium heat, bring cream and dissolved espresso powder to a boil. Remove from heat and add chocolate all at once. Stir until chocolate melts. Add liqueur and strain into a bowl. Keep warm. To serve, soften ice cream for 15–20 minutes at room temperature. Pipe a layer of espresso cream into the bottom of six large wine goblets. Add scoops of ice cream. Spoon over warm chocolate sauce and top with rosette of cream. Serve with remaining sauce.

Chocolate Truffles

Truffles can be simply dusted with cocoa, icing sugar, finely chopped nuts or coated in melted chocolate.

Makes 20 large or
30 medium truffles

INGREDIENTS
250 ml/8 fl oz/1 cup double cream
285 g/10 oz fine quality bittersweet or
　semi-sweet chocolate, chopped
45 g/1½ oz/3 tbsp unsalted butter, cut
　into small pieces
45 ml/1½ fl oz/3 tbsp brandy, whisky
　or other liqueur

TO FINISH (OPTIONAL)
unsweetened cocoa for dusting
finely chopped pistachios
400 g/14 oz bittersweet chocolate

bittersweet
chocolate

brandy

pistachios

cocoa

1 In a saucepan over medium heat, bring cream to a boil. Remove from heat and add chocolate all at once. Stir gently until melted. Stir in butter until melted, then stir in brandy or liqueur. Strain into a bowl and cool to room temperature. Cover and refrigerate for 4 hours or overnight.

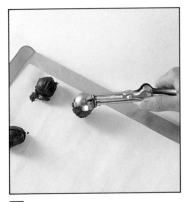

2 Using a small ice cream scoop, melon baller or tablespoon, scrape up mixture into 20 large balls or 30 medium balls and place on a non-stick baking paper-lined baking sheet.

3 If dusting with cocoa, sift a thick layer of cocoa on to a dish or pie plate. Roll truffles in cocoa, rounding them between the palms of your hands. (Dust your hands with cocoa to prevent truffles sticking.) Do not worry if the truffles are not perfectly round as the irregular shape looks more authentic.

4 Alternatively, roll in very finely chopped pistachios. Refrigerate for up to 10 days or freeze for up to 2 months.

5 If coating with chocolate, do not roll in cocoa or nuts, but freeze for 1 hour. Temper the chocolate. Alternatively, truffles can be coated with chocolate melted by the direct heat method if refrigerated immediately. In a small bowl, melt chocolate by either method. Using a fork, dip truffles into melted chocolate, one at a time, tapping fork on edge of bowl to shake off excess. Place on a non-stick baking paper-lined baking sheet. If chocolate begins to thicken, reheat gently until smooth. Refrigerate until set.

Chocolate Fudge Ribbon

This fudge can be stored in an airtight container in the fridge for up to two weeks.

Makes about 48 triangles

INGREDIENTS

600 g/1 lb 5 oz fine quality white chocolate, chopped

1 × 400 ml/14 fl oz tin sweetened condensed milk

15 ml/1 tbsp vanilla essence

7.5 ml/1½ tsp freshly squeezed lemon juice

pinch of salt

215 g/7½ oz/1½ cup hazelnuts or pecans, chopped (optional)

170 g/6 oz semi-sweet chocolate, chopped

45 g/1½ oz/3 tbsp unsalted butter, cut into pieces

55 g/2 oz semi-sweet chocolate, melted, for drizzling

semi-sweet chocolate

vanilla essence

lemon

white chocolate

hazelnuts

1 Line a 20 cm/8 in square baking tin with foil. Oil bottom and sides of foil. In a saucepan over low heat, melt chocolate and condensed milk until smooth, stirring frequently. Remove from heat and stir in vanilla essence, lemon juice and salt; if using, stir in nuts. Spread half the mixture in the tin. Refrigerate for 15 minutes.

2 In a saucepan over low heat, melt chocolate and butter until smooth, stirring frequently. Remove from heat, cool slightly, then pour over chilled white layer and refrigerate for 15 minutes.

3 Gently re-heat remaining white chocolate mixture and pour over set chocolate layer, smooth top, then refrigerate until set, 2–4 hours.

4 Using foil as a guide, remove fudge from pan and turn on to cutting board. Remove foil and with a sharp knife cut into 24 squares. Cut each square into triangles. If you wish, drizzle with melted chocolate.

Chocolate Peppermint Crisps

If you do not have a sugar thermometer, test cooked sugar for 'hard ball stage' by spooning a few drops into a bowl of cold water; it should form a hard ball when rolled between fingers.

Makes 30 crisps

INGREDIENTS
50 g/1¾ oz/¼ cup granulated sugar
65 ml/2 fl oz/¼ cup water
5 ml/1 tsp peppermint essence
250 g/8 oz bittersweet or semi-sweet
   chocolate, chopped

bittersweet chocolate

peppermint essence

1 Lightly brush a large baking sheet with flavourless oil. In a saucepan over medium heat, heat the sugar and water swirling pan gently until sugar dissolves. Boil rapidly until sugar reaches 138°C/280°F on a sugar thermometer (see introduction). Remove pan from heat and add peppermint essence; swirl to blend. Pour on to the baking sheet and allow to set and cool completely.

2 When cold, break into small pieces. Place in a food processor fitted with the metal blade and process until fine crumbs form; do not over-process.

3 Line 2 baking sheets with non-stick baking paper. Place chocolate in a small bowl over a small saucepan of hot water. Place over very low heat until chocolate has melted, stirring frequently until smooth. Remove from heat and stir in peppermint mixture.

4 Using a teaspoon, drop small mounds on to prepared sheets. Using the back of the spoon, spread to 4 cm/1½ in rounds. Cool, then refrigerate to set for about 1 hour. Peel off the paper and store in airtight containers with non-stick baking paper between the layers.

Chocolate Nut Clusters

If you do not possess a sugar thermometer, you can test cooked sugar for 'soft ball stage' by spooning a small amount into a bowl of cold water: it should form a soft ball when rolled between finger and thumb.

Makes about 30

INGREDIENTS
515 ml/18 fl oz/2¼ cups double
  cream
30 g/1 oz/2 tbsp unsalted butter, cut
  into small pieces
350 ml/12 fl oz/1½ cups corn syrup
200 g/7 oz/1 cup granulated sugar
100 g/3½ oz/½ cup (packed) light
  brown sugar
pinch of salt
15 ml/½ fl oz/1 tbsp vanilla essence
420 g/15 oz/3 cups hazelnuts, pecans,
  walnuts, brazil nuts or unsalted
  peanuts, or a combination
400 g/14 oz semi-sweet chocolate,
  chopped
30 g/1 oz/2 tbsp white vegetable fat

1 Lightly oil 2 baking sheets with vegetable oil. In a large heavy-based saucepan over medium heat, cook the cream, butter, corn syrup, sugars and salt, stirring occasionally, until sugars dissolve and butter melts, about 3 minutes. Bring to the boil and continue cooking, stirring frequently, until caramel reaches 120°C/240°F (soft ball stage) on a sugar thermometer, about 1 hour.

2 Place bottom of saucepan into a pan of cold water to stop cooking or transfer caramel to a smaller saucepan. Cool slightly, then stir in vanilla.

3 Stir nuts into caramel until well-coated. Using an oiled tablespoon, drop spoonfuls of nut mixture on to prepared sheets, about 2.5 cm/1 in apart. If mixture hardens, return to heat to soften. Refrigerate clusters for 30 minutes until firm and cold, or leave in a cool place until hardened.

semi-sweet chocolate

brazil nuts

walnuts

hazelnuts

peanuts

pecans

4 Using a metal palette knife, transfer clusters to a wire rack placed over a baking sheet to catch drips. In a medium saucepan, over low heat, melt chocolate and white vegetable fat until smooth, stirring until smooth. Cool slightly.

5 Spoon chocolate over each cluster, being sure to cover completely. Alternatively, using a fork, dip each cluster into chocolate and lift out, tapping on edge of saucepan to shake off excess.

6 Place on a wire rack over a baking sheet. Allow to set for 2 hours until hardened. Store in an airtight container.

Double Chocolate-dipped Fruit

Just about any kind of fruit can be dipped in chocolate as long as the fruit is *dry*: even one drop of moisture can cause the melted chocolate to seize and harden. To store chocolate-dipped fruit for more than 12 hours, the chocolate should be tempered.

Makes 24 coated pieces

INGREDIENTS

fruits – about 24 pieces (strawberries, cherries, orange segments, large seedless grapes, cape gooseberries, kumquats, stoned prunes, stoned dates, dried apricots, dried pears or nuts)

115 g/4 oz fine quality white chocolate, chopped

115 g/4 oz fine quality bittersweet or semi-sweet chocolate, chopped

cherries

grapes

cape gooseberries

strawberries

kumquats

dates

1 Clean and prepare fruits; wipe strawberries with a soft cloth or brush gently with pastry brush. Wash and dry firm-skinned fruits such as cherries and grapes; dry well and set on kitchen paper to absorb any remaining moisture. Peel or cut any other fruits being used. Dried or crystallized fruits can also be used.

2 Melt white chocolate until smooth, stirring frequently. Remove from heat and cool to tepid (about 29°C/84°F), stirring frequently. Line a baking sheet with non-stick baking paper. Holding fruits by the stem or end and at an angle, dip about two-thirds of the fruit into the chocolate. Allow excess to drip off and place on baking sheet. (If chocolate becomes too thick, set over hot water to soften slightly.) Refrigerate fruits until chocolate sets, about 20 minutes.

3 In the top of the cleaned double boiler over low heat, melt the bittersweet or semi-sweet chocolate, stirring frequently until smooth. Remove from heat and cool to just below body temperature, about 30°C/88°F.

4 Take each white chocolate-coated fruit from baking sheet and, holding by the stem or end and at the opposite angle, dip bottom third of each piece into the dark chocolate, creating a chevron effect. Set on baking sheet. Refrigerate for 15 minutes or until set. Remove from refrigerator 10–15 minutes before serving to soften chocolate.

Chocolate Christmas Cups

To crystallize cranberries for decoration, beat an egg white until frothy. Dip each berry first in the egg white then in caster sugar. Place on sheets of non-stick baking paper to dry.

Makes about 35 cups

INGREDIENTS

70–80 foil or paper sweet cases
285 g/10 oz semi-sweet chocolate, broken into pieces
170 g/6 oz cooked, cold Christmas pudding
85 ml/3 fl oz/⅓ cup brandy or whisky
chocolate leaves and crystallized cranberries to decorate

semi-sweet chocolate

brandy

1 Place the chocolate in a medium bowl over a saucepan of hot water. Place saucepan over low heat until chocolate is melted, stirring frequently until chocolate is smooth. Using a pastry brush, brush or coat the bottom and side of about 35 sweet cases. Allow to set, then repeat, reheating melted chocolate if necessary, applying a second coat. Leave to cool and set completely, 4–5 hours or overnight. Reserve remaining chocolate.

2 Crumble the Christmas pudding in a small bowl; sprinkle with brandy or whisky and allow to stand for 30–40 minutes, until brandy is absorbed.

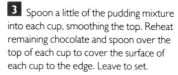

3 Spoon a little of the pudding mixture into each cup, smoothing the top. Reheat remaining chocolate and spoon over the top of each cup to cover the surface of each cup to the edge. Leave to set.

4 When completely set, carefully peel off the cases and place in clean foil cases. Decorate with chocolate leaves and crystallized berries.

Chocolate Box with Caramel Mousse and Berries

Do not add caramel shards too long before serving the Chocolate Box as moisture may cause them to melt.

Serves 8–10

INGREDIENTS
285 g/10 oz semi-sweet chocolate, broken into pieces

CARAMEL MOUSSE
4 × 61.5 g/2 oz chocolate-coated caramel bars, coarsely chopped
20 ml/¾ fl oz/1½ tbsp milk or water
350 ml/12 fl oz/1½ cups double cream
1 egg white

CARAMEL SHARDS
100 g/3½ oz/½ cup granulated sugar
65 ml/2 fl oz/¼ cup water

TOPPING
115 g/4 oz fine quality white chocolate, chopped
350 ml/12 fl oz/1½ cups double cream
450 g/1 lb mixed berries or cut up fruits such as raspberries, strawberries, blackberries or sliced nectarine and orange segments

1 Prepare the chocolate box. Turn a 23 cm/9 in square baking tin bottom-side up. Mould a piece of foil around the tin, then turn it right side up and line it with the foil, pressing against the edges to make the foil as smooth as possible.

2 Place the semi-sweet chocolate in a bowl over a saucepan of hot water. Place saucepan over low heat and stir until chocolate is melted and smooth. Immediately pour melted chocolate into the lined tin and tilt to coat bottom and sides evenly, keeping top edges of sides as straight as possible. As chocolate coats sides, tilt pan again to coat the corners and sides again. Refrigerate until firm, 45 minutes.

3 In a medium bowl, place the caramel bars and milk or water. Place over a pan of hot water over medium heat and stir until melted. Remove from heat and cool for 10 minutes, stirring occasionally. In a bowl with electric mixer, whip cream until soft peaks form. Stir a spoonful of cream into caramel mixture, then fold in remaining cream. In another bowl with electric mixer and cleaned beaters, beat egg white until just stiff; fold into mousse mixture. Pour into the box. Refrigerate for several hours or overnight.

semi-sweet chocolate

raspberries

chocolate bar

strawberries

eggs

white chocolate

4 Meanwhile prepare the caramel shards. Lightly oil a baking sheet. In a small saucepan over low heat, dissolve the sugar in the water, swirling pan gently. Increase the heat and boil mixture until sugar begins to turn a pale golden colour, 4–5 minutes. When mixture is a golden caramel colour, immediately pour onto the oiled sheet, tilt sheet to distribute caramel in an even layer; *do not touch – caramel is dangerously hot.* Cool completely, then using a metal palette knife lift off baking sheet and break into pieces. Set aside to decorate.

5 In a small saucepan over low heat, melt the white chocolate and 125 ml/ 4 fl oz/½ cup cream until smooth, stirring frequently. Strain into a medium bowl and cool to room temperature, stirring occasionally. In another bowl with electric mixer, beat the remaining cream until firm peaks form. Stir a spoonful of cream into the white chocolate mixture, then fold in remaining whipped cream.

Using foil as a guide, remove mousse-filled box from the foil by peeling foil carefully from sides, then bottom. Slide onto serving plate.

6 Spoon chocolate-cream mixture into an icing bag fitted with a medium star tip and pipe a decorative design of rosettes or shells over the surface of the set mousse. Decorate the cream-covered box with the fruits and caramel shards.

Truffle-filled Easter Egg

This is a very fiddly procedure, but the result is very rewarding and makes a welcome gift. The finished egg can be decorated with ribbons.

Makes 1 large, hollow Easter egg

INGREDIENTS
350 g/12 oz plain couverture
   chocolate, tempered, or plain, milk
   or white chocolate, melted
truffles (see Chocolate Truffles recipe
   on page 78)

milk chocolate

plain couverture chocolate

COOK'S TIP

To be sure there are no scratches or rough spots on the chocolate moulds (this would cause chocolate to stick), use a cotton wool ball to polish the insides of two 15 cm/6 in plastic Easter egg moulds.

1 Line a small baking sheet with non-stick baking paper. Using a small ladle or spoon, pour in enough melted chocolate to coat the moulds. Tilt the moulds slowly to coat the sides completely; pour any excess back into the bowl of chocolate and set moulds, open side down, on the prepared baking sheet. Refrigerate for 1–2 minutes until just set.

   Apply second coat of chocolate and refrigerate for 1–3 minutes until set. Repeat a third time and refrigerate for at least 1 hour or until completely set. (Work quickly to avoid having to re-temper chocolate; untempered chocolate can be reheated if it hardens.)

2 To unmould eggs, trim any drops of chocolate from the edge of the mould. Gently insert the point of a small knife between the chocolate and the mould to break the air lock.

3 Holding the mould open side down, squeeze firmly to release the egg half. Repeat with the other half and refrigerate, loosely covered. (Do not touch chocolate surface with fingers as they will leave prints.) Reserve any melted chocolate to reheat for 'glue'.

4 To assemble the egg, hold one half of the egg with a piece of folded kitchen paper or foil and fill with small truffles. If necessary use the remaining melted chocolate as 'glue'. Spread a small amount on to the rim of the egg half and, holding the empty egg half with a piece of kitchen paper or foil, press it on to the filled half, making sure the rims are carefully joined.

5 Hold for several seconds, then prop up egg with the folded paper towel or foil and refrigerate to set. If you like, decorate the egg with ribbons or Easter decorations.

White Chocolate Celebration Cake

The ingredients for the cake mixture make one 30 cm/ 12 in cake. You will need to double the ingredients for the cake and buttercream, preparing each batch separately to ensure even baking. If you wish to make a smaller cake, bake only one layer, and split and fill with one quantity of buttercream and half quantities of lemon syrup and lemon curd.

Serves 40–50

INGREDIENTS
600 g/1 lb 5 oz/4 cups plain flour
10 g/2 tsp bicarbonate of soda
pinch of salt
225 g/8 oz white chocolate, chopped
250 ml/8 fl oz/1 cup whipping cream
225 g/8 oz/1 cup unsalted butter,
    softened
400 g/14 oz/2 cups caster sugar
6 eggs
10 ml/2 tsp lemon essence
grated zest of 1 lemon
335 ml/11 fl oz/1⅓ cups buttermilk
chocolate leaves to decorate

LEMON SYRUP
100 g/3½ oz/½ cup granulated sugar
125 ml/4 fl oz/½ cup water
30 ml/1 fl oz/2 tbsp fresh lemon juice

WHITE CHOCOLATE CREAM CHEESE
    BUTTERCREAM
350 g/12 oz white chocolate, chopped
500 g/18 oz cream cheese, softened
285 g/10 oz/1¼ cup unsalted butter,
    at room temperature
30 ml/2 tbsp fresh lemon juice
2.5 ml/½ tsp lemon essence

LEMON CURD
Follow the recipe on page 42. You
    will need double the quantity.

55–115 g/2–4 oz/4–8 tbsp unsalted
    butter or margarine, softened

COOK'S TIP
When beating in eggs, if mixture appears to curdle, sprinkle over a little flour mixture to bind.

eggs

lemons

fresh flowers

white chocolate

white chocolate leaves

1 Prepare cake layers. Preheat oven to 180°C/350°F/Gas 4. Grease 30 cm/12 in cake tin or springform tin. Line bottom with non-stick baking paper, grease again, then flour lightly.

Into a bowl, sift together flour, bicarbonate of soda and salt, set aside. In a saucepan over medium heat, melt chocolate and cream, stirring until smooth. Set aside to cool.

In a bowl with electric mixer, beat the butter until creamy, then add sugar and beat for 2–3 minutes. Beat in eggs.

Slowly beat in melted chocolate, lemon essence and zest. Alternately, on low speed, add flour in 4 batches and buttermilk in 3 batches, until batter is smooth. Pour into tin. Bake for 1 hour or until cake tester comes out clean. If top browns before centre is cooked, cover with foil.

Remove cake to rack to cool for 10 minutes. Invert cake on to rack and cool completely. When cool, wrap in clear film until ready to assemble. Make second cake in the same way.

2 Prepare syrup. In a small saucepan, combine sugar and water. Over medium heat bring to a boil, stirring until sugar dissolves. Remove from heat, stir in lemon juice and cool completely. Store in an airtight container. Prepare the lemon curd as instructed on page 42, and cover with clear film.

3 Prepare buttercream. Place chocolate in a bowl over a pan of hot water over low heat and stir until melted. (Do not allow chocolate to become too hot, remove from heat if necessary, then return for further melting.) Cool slightly. In a bowl with electric mixer, beat cream cheese until smooth. Gradually beat in cooled white chocolate, then butter, lemon juice and essence. Refrigerate until ready to use.

4 To assemble, split each cake in half. Spoon syrup over each layer, allowing it to soak in, then repeat. Spread bottom half of each cake with lemon curd and replace top layers. Gently beat buttercream until creamy. Spread a quarter over the top of one of the filled cakes. Place the second filled cake on top. Spread a small amount of softened butter over top and sides to create a smooth, crumb-free surface. Refrigerate for 15 minutes to set.

5 Place cake on serving plate. Reserving a quarter of the buttercream for piping, spread remaining buttercream over top and sides of the cake. Spoon reserved buttercream into a large icing bag fitted with a small star tip and pipe a shell pattern around edges of the cake. Decorate with chocolate leaves and fresh flowers.

Chocolate Christmas Log

Begin preparations for this cake at least one day ahead.
It is easy to prepare, but has several components.
Make the mushrooms by sandwiching small meringues
together with ganache frosting.

Serves 12–14

INGREDIENTS
5 eggs, separated
20 g/¾ oz/3 tbsp unsweetened cocoa
  plus extra for dusting
⅛ tsp cream of tartar
115 g/4 oz/1 cup icing sugar

CHOCOLATE GANACHE FROSTING
300 ml/10 fl oz/1¼ cups double or
  whipping cream
350 g/12 oz bittersweet chocolate,
  chopped
30 ml/2 tbsp brandy or chocolate-
  flavour liqueur

CRANBERRY CHRISTMAS SAUCE
450 g/1 lb fresh or frozen cranberries,
  rinsed and picked over
285 g/10 oz/1 cup seedless raspberry
  preserve, melted
100 g/3½ oz/½ cup granulated sugar,
  or to taste

WHITE CHOCOLATE CREAM FILLING
200 g/7 oz fine quality white
  chocolate, chopped
450 ml/16 fl oz/2 cups double cream
30 ml/2 tbsp brandy or chocolate-
  flavour liqueur (optional)

raspberry preserve

bittersweet
chocolate

cranberries

COOK'S TIP

Small decorative 'mushrooms' are
traditionally used to enhance the
chocolate yule log. These can be
made from meringue. Pipe the 'caps'
and 'stems' separately, and when dry
and hard, stick together using a little
ganache or melted chocolate. You
may lightly dust them with cocoa after
assembling.

1 Prepare ganache frosting. In a
medium saucepan over medium heat,
bring the cream to a boil. Remove from
heat and add chocolate all at once, stirring
constantly until melted and smooth. Stir in
liqueur if using, then strain into a medium
bowl and cool to room temperature.
Remove 125 ml/4 fl oz/½ cup at room
temperature, then refrigerate remaining
ganache for 6–8 hours or overnight.

2 Prepare sauce. In a food processor
fitted with a metal blade, process the
cranberries until liquid. Press through a
sieve into a small bowl, discard pulp. Stir
in melted raspberry preserve and sugar
to taste. If sauce is too thick, add a little
water to thin. Refrigerate until needed.

3 Prepare cake. Preheat oven to 200°C/
400°F/Gas 6. Grease 39 cm × 26 cm/15½
× 10½ in Swiss roll tin, line with non-stick
baking paper, overlapping edge by
2.5 cm/1 in.
  In a bowl with electric mixer, beat egg
yolks until thick and creamy. Reduce
speed and beat in cocoa and half the
sugar. In large bowl with electric mixer
with cleaned beaters, beat egg whites.
Add cream of tartar and beat on high
speed until soft peaks form. Add
remaining sugar 30 ml/2 tbsp at a time,
beating well after each addition until stiff
and glossy. Gently fold beaten yolk
mixture into the whites. Spread batter in
tin and bake for 15–20 minutes.
  Lay a clean dish towel on a work
surface and cover with non-stick baking
paper; dust with cocoa or sugar. When
cake is done, immediately turn out on to
paper. Peel off lining paper. Cut off crisp
edges and, starting from one narrow end,
roll cake with the paper and towel, Swiss
roll fashion. Cool cake.

4 Prepare filling. In a saucepan over low heat, melt white chocolate with 125 ml/4 fl oz/½ cup cream until melted, stirring frequently. Strain into a bowl and cool to room temperature. In another bowl with electric mixer, beat remaining cream and brandy until soft peaks form. Stir a spoonful of cream into white chocolate mixture to lighten it, then fold in remaining cream. Unroll cooled cake and spread with chocolate cream. Starting from the same end, re-roll cake without paper (it doesn't matter if it cracks). Cut off one-quarter at an angle. Place against the long piece to resemble a branch.

5 Allow frosting to soften at room temperature. With an electric mixer, beat the ganache until it begins to lighten in colour and texture, about 30–45 seconds. It should have a soft spreading consistency; do not over-beat as chocolate will become stiff and grainy. Using a metal palette knife, spread ganache over the cake surface. Using a fork, mark the ganache lengthwise to resemble tree bark. Dust cake with icing sugar and serve with cranberry sauce.

Death by Chocolate

There are many versions of this cake; this is a very rich one which is ideal for a large party, as it can serve up to twenty chocolate lovers.

Serves 18–20

INGREDIENTS

225 g/8 oz fine quality bittersweet
   chocolate, chopped
115 g/4 oz/½ cup unsalted butter, cut
   into pieces
170 ml/5½ fl oz/⅔ cup water
250 g/8¾ oz/1¼ cups granulated
   sugar
10 ml/2 tsp vanilla essence
2 eggs, separated
170 ml/5½ fl oz/⅔ cup buttermilk or
   soured cream
265 g/12½ oz/2 cups plain flour
10 ml/2 tsp baking powder
5 ml/1 tsp bicarbonate of soda
pinch of cream of tartar
chocolate curls
raspberries and icing sugar to
   decorate (optional)

CHOCOLATE FUDGE FILLING

450 g/1 lb fine quality couverture
   chocolate or bittersweet chocolate,
   chopped
225 g/8 oz/1 cup unsalted butter
85 ml/3 fl oz/⅓ cup brandy or rum
215 ml/7½ oz/¾ cup seedless
   raspberry preserve

CHOCOLATE GANACHE GLAZE

250 ml/8 fl oz/1 cup double cream
225 g/8 oz couverture chocolate or
   bittersweet chocolate, chopped
30 ml/2 tbsp brandy

chocolate curls

bittersweet
chocolate

eggs

raspberries

1 Preheat oven to 180°C/350°F/Gas 4. Grease a 25 cm/10 in springform tin and line base with non-stick baking paper. In a saucepan over medium-low heat, heat chocolate, butter and water until melted, stirring frequently. Remove from heat, beat in sugar and vanilla and cool.

In a bowl, beat yolks lightly, then beat into cooled chocolate mixture; gently fold in buttermilk or soured cream. Into a bowl, sift flour, baking powder and bicarbonate of soda, then fold into chocolate mixture. In a bowl with an electric mixer, beat egg whites and cream of tartar until stiff peaks form; fold in chocolate mixture.

2 Pour mixture into prepared tin and bake for 45–50 minutes until cake begins to shrink away from side of tin. Remove to a wire rack to cool for 10 minutes (cake may sink in centre, this is normal). Run a sharp knife around the edge of tin, then unclip tin and carefully remove side. Invert cake on to wire rack, remove bottom of tin and cool completely. Wash and dry tin.

3 Prepare filling. In a saucepan over medium heat, heat chocolate, butter and 60 ml/4 tbsp brandy until melted, stirring frequently. Remove from heat and set aside to cool and thicken. Cut cake crosswise into three even layers. Heat the raspberry preserve and remaining brandy until melted and smooth, stirring frequently. Spread a thin layer over each of the cake layers and allow to set.

4 When the filling is spreadable, place the bottom cake layer back in the tin. Spread with half the filling, top with the second layer of cake, then spread with the remaining filling and top with the top cake layer, preserve side down. Gently press layers together, cover and refrigerate for 4–6 hours or overnight.

5 Carefully run a sharp knife around edge of cake to loosen, then unclip and remove side of tin. Set cake on wire rack over a baking sheet to catch any drips. In a medium saucepan, bring the cream to the boil. Remove from heat and add chocolate all at once, stirring until melted and smooth. Stir in the brandy and strain into a bowl. Allow to stand for 4–5 minutes to thicken slightly.

6 Beginning from the centre of the bowl and working out towards the edge, whisk the glaze until smooth and shiny. Pour over the cake using a metal palette knife to help smooth top and sides; allow glaze to set. Slide cake on to serving plate and decorate with chocolate curls and raspberries. Dust with icing sugar. Do not refrigerate glaze or it will become dull.

INDEX